basic Guitar
Workout

D0416396

Other titles by David Mead available from Sanctuary Publishing:

Basic Chords For Guitar
Basic Scales For Guitar
100 Tips For Acoustic Guitar You Should Have Been Told
100 Tips For Blues Guitar You Should Have Been Told
100 Guitar Tips You Should Have Been Told
Rhythm – A Step By Step Guide To Understanding Rhythm For Guitar
10 Minute Guitar Workout
Chords & Scales For Guitarists

With Martin Taylor
Kiss And Tell – Autobiography Of A Travelling Musician

Published by **SMT**®
an imprint of Bobcat Books Limited
14-15 Berners Street, London W1T 3LJ, UK.

Exclusive Distributors:
Music Sales Limited
Distribution Centre, Newmarket Road,
Bury St Edmunds, Suffolk IP33 3YB, UK.
Music Sales Corporation
257 Park Avenue South, New York, NY10010, USA.
Music Sales Pty Limited
20 Resolution Drive, Caringbah, NSW 2229, Australia.

Order No. SMT1518R
ISBN 978-1-86074-369-2
© Copyright 2003 David Mead
published under exclusive licence by SMT, an imprint and registered trade mark of
Bobcat Books Limited, part of The Music Sales Group.

The Author hereby asserts his/her right to be identified as the author of this work in
accordance with Sections 77 to 78 of the Copyright, Designs and Patents Act 1988.

All rights reserved. No part of this book may be reproduced in any form or by any electronic or
mechanical means, including information storage or retrieval systems, without permission in
writing from the publisher, except by a reviewer, who may quote brief passages.
Every effort has been made to trace the copyright holders of the photographs in this book but one
or two were unreachable. We would be grateful if the photographers concerned would contact us.

Printed in the EU.

A catalogue record for this book is available from the British Library.

www.musicsales.com

basic Guitar
Workout

THE LEARNING CENTRES
ACC No. RM6316
DATE 6.12.12
CLASS 787.87 MEA

David Mead

CONTENTS

INTRODUCTION

A few years ago, I wrote a book called *10 Minute Guitar Workout* which acknowledged the fact that time is in very short supply to the practising guitarist in a world full of distractions like earning a living, running a home and generally functioning amidst the chaos of modern life. I borrowed the idea for the book from a Canadian Air Force fitness-training manual with which I had managed to trim a few pounds from my physically idle, desk-bound frame at the cost of only ten minutes daily. I judged that many of the book's aims could be readily transferred to the guitar and set about constructing exercises that would have enough cumulative bite to bring about a high level of technical proficiency amongst my busier pupils with very little time investment on their part. *10 Minute Guitar Workout* set out a practice routine that consisted of graduated and musically wholesome exercises with which the reader would spend ten minutes daily, progressing from chart to chart until their technique had reached a level where most things were – technically, at least – within their grasp. The exercises also contained a lot of subliminal information about music, ensuring that the ear wasn't left undeveloped.

basic Guitar Workout is also dedicated to the task of providing a set of concise practice routines, but in this book you can employ random choice to make up a daily workout regime by choosing one exercise from each of the book's three chapters and playing through them in the time allotted. Each day will produce a different combination of exercises, ensuring that your practice routine will always include fresh challenges to guarantee that your technical development on the guitar remains high gain, interesting and streamlined.

David Mead

QUICK-START WORKOUT

I'm as bad as anyone for not reading instructions, so I'm going to sum up the essence of the next section, 'How To Use This Book', in just a few paragraphs so that you can get started as soon as possible. However, if you've got a few minutes to read the full monty next door, please take the time to do so. The real benefits of the basic workout only become apparent if all of the guidelines are followed to the letter. But for now, let battle commence...

Choose an exercise from Chapter 1 at random – use a pin, divining rod, the fickle finger of fate, anything you like – and follow the instructions for that specific exercise. Don't spend any longer on the exercise than two minutes. Now take a look at the chart below:

Standard	Number Of Repeats In Two Minutes
Beginner	14–26
Intermediate	27–40
Advanced	41–74

For instance, in this example, you should repeat the exercise from 14–26 times in two minutes if you qualify as a beginner, 27–40 times if you're intermediate and 41–74 times if you've reached the heady heights of advanced. The most important thing is to spend only the allotted time on each exercise. Once the time has elapsed, it's gone; the exercise is finished. Even if you didn't make the quota, don't spend any extra time working it out; move on to Chapter 2, reset your stopwatch and pick another exercise at random.

Repeat the procedure for each chapter, choosing at random each time. Once your six-minute routine has finished, get on with anything you want. Next time you sit and practise, pick another three exercises at random. Mathematically, it's going to be a long time before you come around to the same three exercises in the same practice routine again. (In fact, if anyone out there happens to be a maths genius and wants to work out exactly how many combinations there are available, email me at info@davidmead.net and we'll laugh about it together.)

Another important thing is to do the exercises in order: Chapters 1, 2 and 3. This form of mixing and matching is ideal for introducing the random factor into your initial warm-up and technical development. It will serve to constantly challenge you if you attempt the exercises in the time set and should never become stale or predictable. I like to think of it as a kind of guitar *I Ching*. Good luck!

Key To Notation

There's nothing radically new in this book, from a notational point of view. I've tried to make things as simple and as traditional as I can, but just in case you're not wholly familiar with the way in which guitar music tends to be written down, I've included the following guide.

Chord Boxes

Chord boxes are represented by a grid system like the one shown here:

basic Guitar Workout

In the diagram overleaf, the guitar fretboard is represented by six vertical lines, as a guitar would appear if it was leaning against a wall and facing you. So the strings go from left to right, bass to treble, like this:

E A D G B E

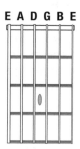

Finger positions are represented by black circles, like the ones shown below:

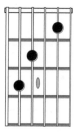

The example here is of a chord of C major, and the diagram calls for you to place a finger on the fifth string at the third fret, on the fourth string at the second fret and on the second string at the first fret. If a string is meant to be omitted from a chord, a small 'x' is written on top of the string concerned, like this:

On the other hand, if an open (unfretted) string is meant to be included in the chord, it will be shown by a small 'o' over the string, as shown here:

basic Guitar Workout

If a chord is to be played down at the nut end of the fretboard, this is represented by a thick line at the top of the strings, like this:

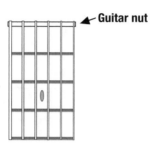

◄━ **Guitar nut**

If the chord is to be played further up the fretboard, away from the nut, a fret number is shown by the side of the chord box:

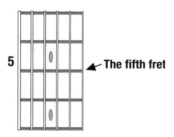

◄━ **The fifth fret**

Any further information necessary to a particular exercise will be pointed out in the accompanying text.

Tablature

Tablature is a dedicated system of notation that has been around for around 400 years or so. There are examples of early tablature in the British Museum representing lute music drawn from the Baroque era. So *tab*, as it's known to its friends, is anything but contemporary and new fangled. Historically, tab faded from common usage due to the waning popularity of the lute and the fact that its 'closed system' of representing notes meant that composers unfamiliar with the workings of the instrument couldn't write for it. Also, it meant that guitarists who were fully conversant with tab had problems communicating with other non-guitar-playing musicians who read only standard notation.

The guitar's return to popularity commenced at the beginning of the 20th century, when classical virtuosi like Tarrega, Pujol, Segovia, Bream and Williams proved that the guitar should be taken seriously by a musical establishment that suffered from the misconception that any instrument that was not part of an orchestra had to have something seriously dodgy about it. So the deal was that, if the guitar wanted to be a proper instrument, it had to toe the line, as far as notation was concerned, and so standard musical notation became mandatory.

It was only during the '60s, when the rise of the electric guitar to popular acclaim seemed inevitable, that tab enjoyed a kind of rebirth. It was greeted with considerable suspicion by the musical fraternity and dubbed a cop-out, sometimes being compared – somewhat haughtily – to painting by numbers. However, if the guitar surged to popularity during the '60s, by the '80s it was unstoppable and, once again, guitar music was mapped out using tablature – alongside standard notation, just to keep music publishers happy. In this book, I have used tablature exclusively in order to make things as universally accessible as possible. If tab has one serious shortfall, however, it is that it conveys no rhythmic information. If, during the course of these exercises, I have designed something to be played to a specific rhythm, I've tried to make it as clear as possible in the accompanying text – a compromise that's still easier than learning to read music, let me tell you.

Reading Tab

For the uninitiated, tablature is represented by six horizontal lines, each representing a string of the guitar:

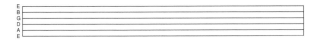

Fret locations are shown by numbers, like the example below:

This example tells you that you're required to play the note at the fifth fret on the G string. If two notes are meant to be played simultaneously, they're stacked vertically, like this:

Here, you're being directed to play the notes found on the G string at the fifth fret and on the B string at the sixth fret. Whole chords are simply written as bigger stacks of numbers, like this:

The chord above is C major, which probably looks more familiar when shown as a chord box:

C major

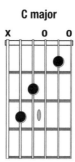

Fretboard Diagrams

Occasionally, information concerning scales or melodies can be more readily conveyed via a similar system to chord boxes. This system provides us with a very useful cross-reference to tablature. As an instrument, the guitar is very 'shape friendly'; we've all spent long hours trying to memorise chord shapes, usually with great and enduring success. By the same token, it's possible to 'see' scale shapes far more clearly when they're represented by an overall pattern, like this:

When both tab and a fretboard diagram are shown as part of an exercise, use the fingering and directions contained in the tablature and treat the fretboard diagram as a kind of bird's-eye view of the situation.

HOW TO USE THIS BOOK

One of the biggest problems facing anyone learning a musical instrument today is knowing how to spend their time in the practice room in the most beneficial way. Without guidance from a teacher, this time tends to be taken up by a lot of people by playing everything in their current repertoires – a catalogue of favourite licks and party tricks, for instance. The natural tendency is to steer well clear of anything that challenges you and takes you further with your playing. Playing the material that you've already got under your fingers will only do you a certain amount of good. In order to maintain the bite that practice should offer, you have to be prepared to take regular leaps into the dark.

Then there's the boredom factor. The same old practice routine will soon lose its effect when the mind starts to wander. That's when autopilot clicks in and takes over, resulting in an emotionless reading of whatever it is you're attempting to play.

This book is aimed at keeping your practice time fresh

by introducing a random factor that wouldn't otherwise be present. The exercises are split into three chapters, each addressing a different area of technical or musical development.

Chapter 1 deals with those all-important first few minutes when you warm up your hands and kick-start your brain into action.

Chapter 2 addresses co-ordination and comes complete with a set of routines designed to challenge both your left and right hands.

Chapter 3 introduces the subject of ear training. All exercises here contain essential information for the ears, with the focus on developing the musical side of your playing.

The idea is to take one exercise from each section every day, choosing each entirely at random, then spending two minutes on each exercise before moving on to the next and then getting on with the rest of your practice routine. The odds on you choosing the same three exercises on two consecutive days are stacked somewhat astronomically against you. In fact, you'll probably never have the same three exercises in your practice routine, which means that the unpredictability of the whole thing should keep everything interesting and fresh for a long time to come. You'll be able to mark your progress by keeping your eye on the number of times that you can manage to repeat each exercise in the two minutes allowed, too, and so there's the extra incentive of continuous challenge to spur you on to maintain the course.

Good Practice Habits

I thought it would be a good idea at this point to spend a few minutes talking about practice in general and offer a couple of dos and don'ts.

Posture

It's a fact (although not a particularly well-publicised one) that guitarists tend to suffer from back problems and that a lot of these problems stem from bad posture, either in performance or in the practice room. Just a few minutes' thought will convince you that the human body and the guitar weren't exactly made for each other, from a high-level ergonomic point of view. The kinds of demands that the instrument imposes on the performer in terms of posture and hand positions alone are enough to wave a red flag to any physiotherapist. So what can we, as musicians, do to stay out of the chiropractor's clutches? For a start, adopting a simple checklist before any playing or practising is a good idea.

- When playing, sit in a straight-backed chair with adequate back support. Practising while slumped on the sofa is a complete no-no.

- Try to keep your back as straight as possible and not curved. Basically, don't slouch!

- Keep both of your wrists as straight as possible.

- Try to eliminate tension from your arms and hands. Tension actually prevents free movement and can inhibit progress. If you feel yourself tensing up, try to consciously relax for a few minutes before continuing.

If at any time you experience aches and pains, fizziness or pins and needles in your hands or wrists, stop playing and rest, then take a good look at your playing position before continuing. If symptoms persist, see a doctor specialising in sport or performance therapy. I once contracted a touch of tendonitis (inflammation of the tendons in the arm or wrist) from playing pinball on a games console and had to stop playing guitar for a while to make sure that I didn't do myself any lasting damage. (I also had to give up playing virtual pinball, which was a pity, because I was getting some really impressive scores.) It's surprising just how easy it is to place your playing in danger. I was caught out. Don't let it happen to you!

Guitar Straps

It's implausible to practise while sitting down in one playing position and then expect to be able to stand up and play in another, totally different position and expect the same results. For the best results, you've really got to adopt one playing position and stick with it, no matter what. One way around this problem is to wear a guitar strap that has been adjusted so that it keeps the guitar in the same basic position while you're either sitting or standing. In this way, the absolute minimum adjustment is necessary and you'll avoid those awful moments on gigs where some tricky passage you've mastered in the practice room suddenly turns into an untamed beast onstage for no apparent reason. If your guitar is fairly heavy, make sure that you buy a strap wide enough to distribute the weight evenly across your shoulder. A hefty guitar hanging from your shoulder on something the width of a shoestring is a recipe for disaster! Think cheesewire...

The Practice Environment

The geography of many modern houses, combined with contemporary family life in general, makes it very difficult for the average player to have a dedicated music room, but your practice environment is very important, nonetheless. Practising in the corner of the living room while the rest of the family tries to watch TV and shoots black looks at you isn't a healthy situation to be in at all. Practice is all about focus, and that's just not possible if any major distractions are allowed to intrude.

Try to pick a time when the family bustle is at a minimum and literally steal a few calm moments for yourself and your guitar. Obviously, if your practice is to have the most effect, it needs to be regular. When I was teaching full time, I could easily pick out the pupils who had taken my advice and done a little practice every day from the ones who had reintroduced themselves to their instrument for about 30 minutes before leaving to come for their lesson! With the latter, we ended up covering the same ground week after week, the excuse being that lack of time was the villain of the piece. But the fact was that I had far busier pupils who managed to squeeze ten minutes or so of practice into their schedules, and they progressed much faster than their once-a-week's-enough fellow students. The moral of this story (and, indeed, this entire book) is that, when it comes to practice, little and often is far better and more effective than 30 minutes once a fortnight.

Warm-ups First

Whatever you do, spend a little time letting your hands warm up at the beginning of each session. Warm-ups are built into the exercises in Chapter 1 of this book (another reason why the exercises should all be done in order), so no further limbering should be necessary. If you think of your hands as athletes, you wouldn't want them to run 2,000 metres without any preparation. Similarly, doing some gentle stretching – the equivalent of slowly going up through the gears – will make sure that everything's ticking over nicely by the time you come to tackling the remainder of your practice schedule.

I also heartily recommend that you fork out for a music stand as soon as possible. They are sound investments, as they're relatively cheap and readily available at all good music stores, and buying one will save you an awful lot of frustration and potential eyestrain. Obviously, the bulk of your practice time is going to be spent reading music, tab transcriptions or tutor books like this one, and using a music stand is really heaps better than trying to balance a music book on your knee or trying to read one that you've lodged on the floor. When you sit and practise, it's best to try to rule out as many potential irritations as is humanly possible, and pages flapping about just when you've got to the good bit of a transcription or, worse, books falling on the floor can be easily dealt with by using a music stand.

Continuity

If, for any reason, you have to break off from a progressive practice routine (like the one outlined in this book) for any length of time, you'll probably find that it's a struggle to get back to where you left off. My advice here is not to try. Take a few paces back and start at a slightly lower level or a slower pace and bring yourself back up to speed gradually.

The Exercises

All of the exercises in this book have been designed for alternate picking, unless otherwise noted. Alternate picking means that a downstroke with the pick or plectrum is followed by an upstroke consecutively throughout. You should pay special attention to your right-hand position when attempting fast alternate picking. Make sure that there is minimum tension in the arm and wrist. Tension slows you down and can cause repetitive strain injury and, as such, is definitely something you want to lose during the early stages of building speed into your playing. Don't allow the wrist or hand to become rigid under any circumstances and don't be tempted to clench into a fist those fingers not concerned with picking. None of the exercises contained in this book call for any Olympic standards and should all fall within the capabilities of the intermediate-to-advanced player.

Timing

The best advice I can give anyone about timing is to buy a metronome or a cheap drum machine, anything that will act as a 'pacer' while you practise. This will help you develop a good sense of rhythm and a general 'feel' for music. Rhythm has an effect over such things as phrasing and many other essential elements that all combine to make up an overall musical style. If you pay sufficient attention to rhythmic training early enough, it will become part of your natural musicianship as a matter of course, saving you time later on when you realise that perhaps timing is not your forte. I've known pupils finding it difficult to play along with a metronome taking the simple option of practising without one, only to realise later on that they can't play in time with a drummer or backing track! They didn't realise that it's exactly the same thing – if you can play in time with a metronome, you can play in time with just about anything. Yes, it's yet another thing to learn, but it's an exceedingly valuable one, so don't encourage any 'square wheels' in your playing by leaving this essential musical element undeveloped. The small cost of a metronome will pay you back 1,000 times as your musical instincts begin to form.

1 WARM-UPS

The purpose of the exercises in this initial section is to pose a physical and mental conundrum to kick-start the brain and fingers at the beginning of your practice session. The workouts here constitute a gentle assault course for the fingers on the left hand. Some are designed to stretch the hand's span slightly, while most will test your right-hand picking abilities, too. Each exercise has its own set of instructions, but the general rules are that the workout should be repeated for two minutes. The table at the bottom of the page lays down guidelines for how many times you should aim to repeat each exercise, depending on whether you're playing at a beginner's, intermediate or advanced player's level.

The watchword here, in all instances, is accuracy over speed. It's no good claiming that you've reached the rarefied realm of the advanced if the exercise is fractured, blurred or just plain erratic. It's far better for you as a musician to accept a lower speed at 100% crystal-clear accuracy. Good luck!

WORKOUT 1

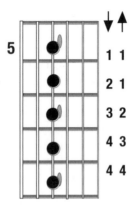

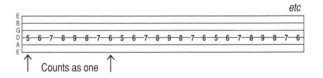

Counts as one

etc

What You Do

This is a chromatic exercise on the D string, but it covers five frets. This happens a lot in guitar music – four fingers have to cope with five frets. Two different fingerings appear in the exercise: the fourth finger plays the extra note on the way up and the first finger steps in on the return journey.

Points To Watch

Make sure that your fingering is as shown in the diagram and ensure that your right-hand picking is strictly alternate.

How It Benefits You

This exercise is all about gently nudging the left hand into action. It's not a race; the number of repeats allows for quite an easy time of things at all levels!

Standard	Number Of Repeats In Two Minutes
Beginner	30–50
Intermediate	51–100
Advanced	101–120

WORKOUT 2

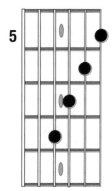

5

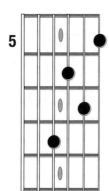

5

What You Do

This exercise has two chord shapes at the fifth fret, and all you have to do is change between them. You'll notice that it's only fingers 2 and 3 that are called on to move. Keep fingers 1 and 4 on the fretboard while this happens.

Points To Watch

Make sure that your left hand doesn't become tense – it needs to be as relaxed as possible. It doesn't matter if you pick or pluck this exercise, so feel free to follow your inclinations in this respect.

How It Benefits You

The third finger is notorious for not having a lot of independent movement, and this exercise should help things. You'll find it hard to begin with, but it will ease up as the fingers gain more freedom of movement.

Standard	Number Of Repeats In Two Minutes
Beginner	40–80
Intermediate	81–140
Advanced	141–160

WORKOUT 3

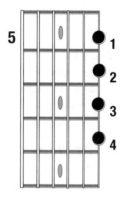

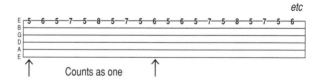

Counts as one

What You Do

Here is a chromatic exercise on the top E string. The fingers of the left hand alternate with the first finger to play over a four-fret span.

Points To Watch

Make sure that the exercise is performed accurately, with an equally clear and rhythmically accurate note from each finger. Watch the picking, too – it should be strictly alternate!

How It Benefits You

Basically, this exercise ensures that all four fretting fingers are performing well.

Standard	Number Of Repeats In Two Minutes
Beginner	10–48
Intermediate	49–70
Advanced	71–100

WORKOUT 4

5    **5**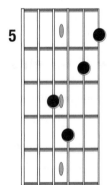

What You Do

Two chords shapes here to change between, but it's only the third and fourth fingers that actually move. The rest of the hand remains still.

Points To Watch

Make sure that fingers 1 and 2 stay on the neck while fingers 3 and 4 swap positions. Don't let tension build up in the hand.

How It Benefits You

Fingers 3 and 4 were never really meant to be able to move as freely and as independently as is necessary for playing guitar. This exercise should start oiling the cogs!

Standard	Number Of Repeats In Two Minutes
Beginner	40–80
Intermediate	81–100
Advanced	101–140

WORKOUT 5

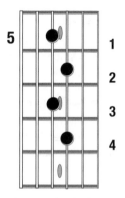

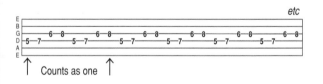

What You Do

This is an exercise that calls for left-hand finger movement over two strings. Position the fingers one finger per fret before you begin and try to keep the fingers in position at all times.

Points To Watch

You're picking across two strings here, so be careful to ensure that picking remains alternate. You might find at first that you don't really know where to look. If in doubt, work with the left hand and make sure it's learnt what it has to do before trying to pick.

How It Benefits You

Picking across strings catches out a lot of people, especially if the left hand is doing something tricky at the same time. This exercise will break you in nicely.

Standard	Number Of Repeats In Two Minutes
Beginner	20–60
Intermediate	61–96
Advanced	97–120

WORKOUT 6

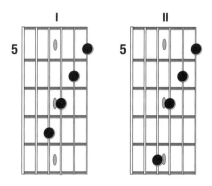

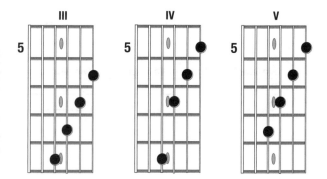

What You Do

Here's a real test for the flexibility of the left hand. This exercise requires you to stretch your fourth finger by having it shift a whole fret up the neck by itself before the rest of the hand catches it up. This might seem very difficult to achieve, to begin with, so take things slowly.

Points To Watch

Try to make sure that the fourth finger moves independently, if possible. If not, feel free to lift the fingers of the left hand while finger 4 makes its move.

How It Benefits You

Making a man of that fourth finger is the name of the game here. Take care not to push things too far; this is one of the more demanding warm-ups. (Note: timings are set for the completion of all five chord shapes.)

Standard	Number Of Repeats In Two Minutes
Beginner	5–20
Intermediate	21–40
Advanced	41–60

WORKOUT 7

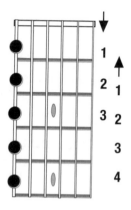

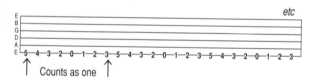

Counts as one

What You Do

Here's a chromatic exercise down at the bottom end of the fretboard. Basically, you play five fretted notes plus the open string.

Points To Watch

The open string here will catch you out in the initial stages, as will the asymmetric left-hand fingering. Watch your picking to make sure it remains alternate and aim for good clean accuracy all round.

How It Benefits You

This calls for one of the biggest stretches on the guitar – you're down at the bottom of the fretboard and playing on the bass string, so to begin with it might feel a little like running on soft sand.

Standard	Number Of Repeats In Two Minutes
Beginner	10–24
Intermediate	25–60
Advanced	61–80

WORKOUT 8

I

II

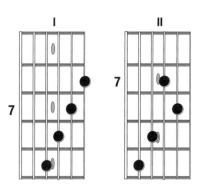

III

IV

V

What You Do

Here are two chord shapes calling for two fingers to swap position, moved across the fingerboard! This really is diabolical at first, as it calls for several movements at once.

Points To Watch

You'll need to check and recheck that your fingers are swapping at the right place (in mid-air, not on the fretboard) as you move to and fro.

How It Benefits You

If you've ever experienced difficulties when changing chords, this exercise should be like six weeks on manoeuvres with the Marines! Basically, if you manage to get this one up and running, changing between 'normal' chords should never faze you again. (Note: one complete cycle of this workout is represented by changing between positions I, II, III and IV. Position V is always the start of a new cycle.)

Standard	Number Of Repeats In Two Minutes
Beginner	10–25
Intermediate	26–50
Advanced	51–70

WORKOUT 9

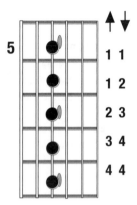

5

1 1
1 2
2 3
3 4
4 4

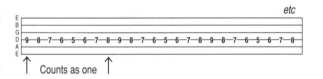

etc

↑ Counts as one ↑

What You Do

This is chromatic series of five notes that requires your left hand to shift position so that it can cover the span necessary. Cunningly enough, it begins on the fourth finger, the weakest...

Points To Watch

Pay special attention to the fingering shown in the diagram. You're expected to play two notes with finger 1 on your way down the neck and two notes with finger 4 at the top. Concentrate on accuracy and precision at all times!

How It Benefits You

Picking, rudimentary co-ordination and deft position changing are all addressed in this exercise.

Standard	Number Of Repeats In Two Minutes
Beginner	30–50
Intermediate	51–100
Advanced	101–120

WORKOUT 10

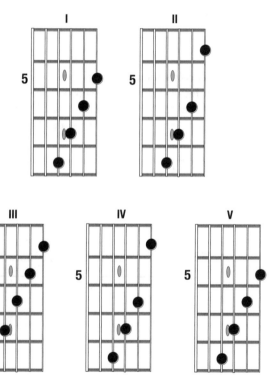

What You Do

A real stretchathon for the first finger, this exercise sees you moving a chord shape down the fingerboard and back up in two parts.

Points To Watch

To begin with, it's going to feel difficult to move your first finger independently of the rest of your left hand, so lessening your grip on the fingerboard while you do so is perfectly OK.

How It Benefits You

Basic flexibility and span are the two prime factors addressed in this workout. Anything that increases the hand's capacity to deal with the rigours of changing chords and position can be considered very worthwhile! (Note: changing between positions I, II, III and IV represent one turn of the exercise. Position V is shown in the diagram for completeness' sake.)

Standard	Number Of Repeats In Two Minutes
Beginner	15–30
Intermediate	31–60
Advanced	61–75

WORKOUT 11

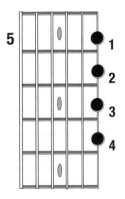

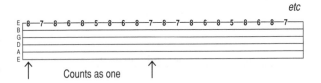

What You Do

Here we have a four-note chromatic series on the top E string. This workout calls for you to alternate between your fourth finger and the rest of the left-hand fingers up and down the four-fret span.

Points To Watch

Your little finger is probably not yet the Ninja warrior it's destined to become, so to begin with this exercise will probably feel like heavy going. Aim for accuracy and leave the question of speed until much later on.

How It Benefits You

The fundamental flexibility and strength of the left hand's weakest member is the all-important factor here. Combined with some accurate right-hand picking from you, this is guaranteed to stimulate the senses!

Standard	Number Of Repeats In Two Minutes
Beginner	10–25
Intermediate	26–50
Advanced	51–100

WORKOUT 12

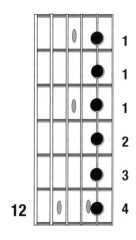

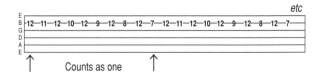

What You Do

Spanning a mighty six frets, this exercise really puts the pressure on the first finger to perform. Line up the four fingers of your fretting hand, as shown, and take extra note of the part that the first finger has to play.

Points To Watch

This exercise will test the willingness of your fourth finger to take orders from your brain! Plus, it's a gentle stretch for the first finger, too. Combine these two elements with some accurate right-hand picking and there's enough technique-developing potential in this workout to last a lifetime.

How It Benefits You

The three elements of picking, increasing the left hand's span and putting pressure on the fourth finger's development make sure that there's a lot to be gained from this workout.

Standard	Number Of Repeats In Two Minutes
Beginner	10–20
Intermediate	21–50
Advanced	51–70

WORKOUT 13

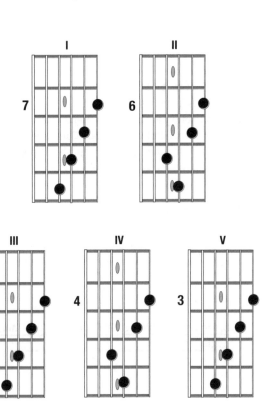

What You Do

Here are five alternating chord positions that descend the guitar neck in an exercise designed to test your chord-changing abilities to the limit! Swapping over the third and fourth fingers shouldn't hold the exercise up or slow things down. Aim for absolute precision and even timing.

Points To Watch

Obviously, this exercises focuses on the weaker fingers of the left hand, and swapping them around will prove difficult to begin with, so you'll have to exercise a lot of patience before everything gels nicely.

How It Benefits You

Both position changing and finger flexibility are addressed in this workout.

Standard	Number Of Repeats In Two Minutes
Beginner	5–24
Intermediate	25–35
Advanced	36–50

WORKOUT 14

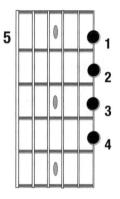

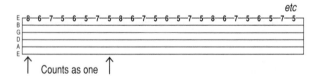

Counts as one

What You Do

This is a straightforward chromatic exercise, covering four frets. Begin on the eighth fret with the fourth finger, aiming for economy of movement in the positioning of the other left-hand fingers. When the exercise is ascending, keep the fingers on the fretboard as much as possible.

Points To Watch

Don't let your left-hand fingers flap around unnecessarily – you don't have to lift them too far from the fretboard. Also, make sure that your right-hand picking is strictly alternate, clean and accurate.

How It Benefits You

Basic co-ordination, independence of the left-hand fingers and accuracy of picking are all taken care of here.

Standard	Number Of Repeats In Two Minutes
Beginner	10–30
Intermediate	31–60
Advanced	61–120

WORKOUT 15

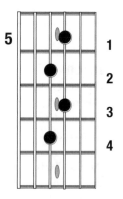

Counts as one

What You Do

In this exercise, you're cross-picking with your right hand and fretting alternate strings with your left.

Points To Watch

Check the basic positions of the left-hand fingers. This simple pattern calls upon your right hand to pick accurately over two strings, so make sure that your left hand knows what it's up to before you begin, because your attention might be initially directed towards your right hand.

How It Benefits You

This exercise is another assault course that addresses basic co-ordination between left and right hands. In fact, it's an excellent wake-up call for your guitar-playing instincts!

Standard	Number Of Repeats In Two Minutes
Beginner	10–40
Intermediate	41–75
Advanced	76–120

WORKOUT 16

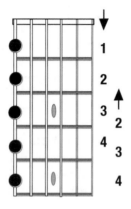

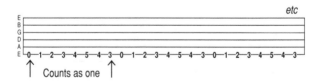

What You Do

This is a chromatic exercise that calls for some serious co-ordination. It covers the first five frets of the bass E string, ensuring that your left hand is at full stretch – as far as routine playing is concerned, at least.

Points To Watch

Study the left-hand fingering carefully. It's different on the way down! To make matters worse, you don't get to complete the cycle each time, as the exercise cuts off after the third fret on the return journey.

How It Benefits You

Here, the span of your left hand is put to the test, as is your ability to make seamless position changes. Many melodic passages on the guitar call for you to play over five frets with four fingers, so this workout should prepare you for this nicely.

Standard	Number Of Repeats In Two Minutes
Beginner	10–30
Intermediate	31–60
Advanced	61–120

WORKOUT 17

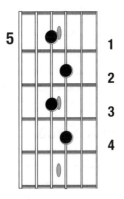

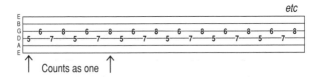

etc

Counts as one

What You Do

This workout covers the normal four-fret left-hand span but over two strings, so your cross-picking skills are being well and truly put to the test.

Points To Watch

Keep your fingers in position as much as possible. Anchor your first and second fingers for the duration of the exercise, employing only the third and fourth fingers to lift and return to the neck each time.

How It Benefits You

This exercise looks at your cross-picking technique and basic co-ordination skills and should do wonders for the independence of the third and fourth fingers on your left hand.

Standard	Number Of Repeats In Two Minutes
Beginner	10–30
Intermediate	31–65
Advanced	66–100

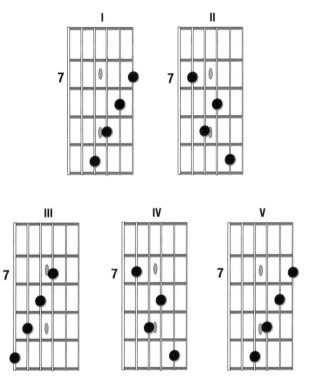

WORKOUT 18

What You Do

Here are four chord shapes that move across the fretboard, with fingers 1 and 4 swapping positions between changes.

Points To Watch

The problem here will be moving the first and fourth fingers without your second and third fingers wanting to move at the same time. Strive to reposition your fingers between chord changes – not on the neck, though, as this will invariably slow things down to a complete halt.

How It Benefits You

This workout should set you up to face even the most awkward chord changes in the guitar-playing repertoire. (Note: the exercise comprises changing between positions I, II, III and IV. Position V is illustrated merely to complete the cycle.)

Standard	Number Of Repeats In Two Minutes
Beginner	8–20
Intermediate	21–30
Advanced	31–100

WORKOUT 19

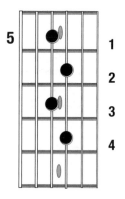

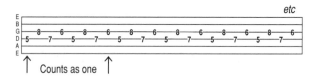

What You Do

This workout combines right-hand cross-picking with a fingering challenge for the left.

Points To Watch

Check the left-hand fingering carefully – it goes 1, 4, 3, 2, which will give you a lot to think about at once while you strive to gain speed. Remember to keep the picking absolutely clean, with no muted notes. Accuracy must come before speed!

How It Benefits You

Any exercise that combines cross-picking with non-straightforward fingering will prepare you for some of music's trickier moments.

Standard	Number Of Repeats In Two Minutes
Beginner	5–15
Intermediate	16–50
Advanced	51–100

WORKOUT 20

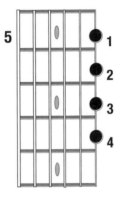

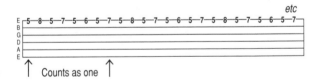

Counts as one

What You Do

Here's a four-note chromatic exercise that calls for some delicate left-hand gymnastics! Finger 1 is anchored at the fifth fret while the other left-hand fingers alternate at their respective fret locations.

Points To Watch

Aim to play this exercise as cleanly as possible. It calls for strict alternate picking in the right hand, while the left-hand fingering might take a while to assimilate.

How It Benefits You

The key word here is precision. The more precise your picking skills become – whatever left-hand fingering you use – the better your overall technique will develop.

Standard	Number Of Repeats In Two Minutes
Beginner	10–20
Intermediate	21–50
Advanced	51–120

WORKOUT 21

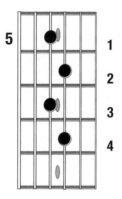

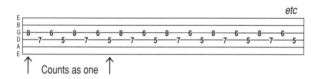

etc

Counts as one

What You Do

This workout requires you to pick over two strings while the left-hand fingers perform a quasi-chromatic descent – hopefully without tying themselves in knots! In this respect, watch the fingering carefully.

Points To Watch

For some reason, any exercise that starts on the left-hand fourth finger feels somehow wrong, so at first this little workout might not fall under the fingers as easily as you'd like. Take care with picking and remember that accuracy will earn you more of a reward than blundering attempts at speed.

How It Benefits You

This will help with simple co-ordination (the real test of which is contained in Chapter 2) and will ensure that all left-hand fingers have an almost equal agility.

Standard	Number Of Repeats In Two Minutes
Beginner	8–15
Intermediate	16–60
Advanced	61–100

WORKOUT 22

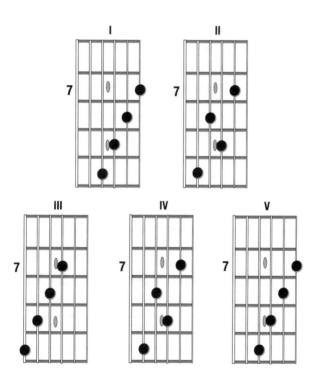

What You Do

In this exercise, a chord shape moves across the fretboard, changing slightly as it does. Fingers 2 and 3 can stay in position, but 1 and 4 have to alternate. Cunning!

Points To Watch

Make sure the fingers swap over between chord changes. Don't try to rearrange your fingers when they're already down on the neck as this will slow things down and ruin the flow. Changes should be even and equal. Use a metronome if necessary.

How It Benefits You

Guitarists spend most of their lives on the bandstand playing chords, so changing smoothly from one to the next is essential, even if it appears severely tricky. This workout will hone your chord-changing skills nicely! (Note: the exercise comprises changing between I, II, III and IV. Position V is illustrated to complete the cycle.)

Standard	Number Of Repeats In Two Minutes
Beginner	10–30
Intermediate	31–45
Advanced	46–65

WORKOUT 23

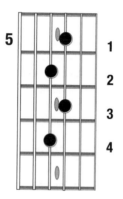

5   1
             2
             3
             4

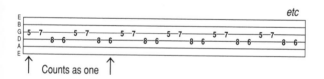

Counts as one

What You Do

Here's a workout to test your co-ordination and picking accuracy! Basically, you're picking two notes per string, ascending on the G string and descending on the D.

Points To Watch

Make sure you understand the left-hand fingering perfectly before attempting to bring this exercise up to speed. It's tricky to begin with, but it shouldn't be anything you can't master after a short time. Pay attention to the right hand, too; try to keep everything as crisp and clean as possible.

How It Benefits You

This is an exercise for working on just about everything – picking, left-hand fluency, etc. The way in which the fourth left-hand finger follows the third is good for gaining independence between these two weaker members of the squad.

Standard	Number Of Repeats In Two Minutes
Beginner	8–15
Intermediate	16–80
Advanced	81–120

WORKOUT 24

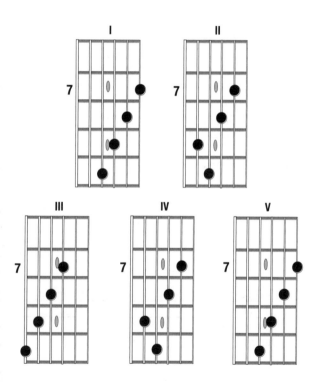

What You Do

Here's an exercise where chord shapes change across groups of strings, with a test of agility for fingers 3 and 4.

Points To Watch

Your third and fourth fingers find it very difficult to move independently of one another – it's actually an anatomical anomaly. However, flexibility can be learned and acquired with exercises like this one. Make sure that you change the fingers around before they come into contact with the strings. Chord changes should morph into position in mid-air, never on the fretboard.

How It Benefits You

However much of a teaser it appears to be, it's possible to master this workout after just a short while. It will do your chord-changing abilities a great deal of good. (Note: The exercise comprises changing between I, II, III and IV. Position V is illustrated to complete the cycle.)

Standard	Number Of Repeats In Two Minutes
Beginner	10–20
Intermediate	21–35
Advanced	36–60

WORKOUT 25

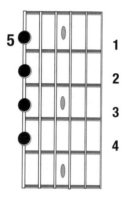

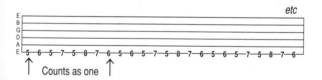

Counts as one

What You Do

Here's a series of four notes on the bass E string that should be played so that all notes alternate with the first left-hand finger on the way up but descend sequentially.

Points To Watch

This workout will stretch the left hand gently, because of the fact that it all takes place with the fingers extended right over to the far edge of the fretboard. This could feel uncomfortable at first – remember, don't overdo things – but should become second nature after just a short while.

How It Benefits You

Playing the guitar calls for the left hand to have equal capacity across the span of the fretboard. In other words, it should feel equally at home while operating on any of the strings. This workout could therefore be seen as essential left-hand orienteering!

Standard	Number Of Repeats In Two Minutes
Beginner	10–25
Intermediate	26–80
Advanced	81–120

WORKOUT 26

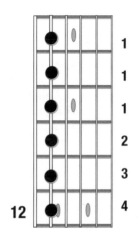

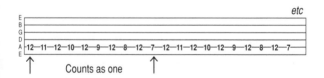

Counts as one

What You Do

Here's a chromatic descent on the A string that calls for
the left hand to span between the 12th and 7th frets,
with finger 1 leading the way. The fourth finger comes
in for some fairly heavy-duty attention, too!

Points To Watch

Try to keep your left hand in one position as far as
possible. Extreme side-to-side movement isn't good,
as it uses energy and can decrease efficiency and
accuracy. Remember, too, the precision-counts-over-
speed principle and take things easy.

How It Benefits You

Any exercise that pushes and develops the left hand's
span slightly will be beneficial in everyday guitar
playing. The fourth finger comes in for its fair share of
attention, too, which will help in building its general
strength and stamina.

Standard	Number Of Repeats In Two Minutes
Beginner	5–12
Intermediate	13–40
Advanced	41–65

WORKOUT 27

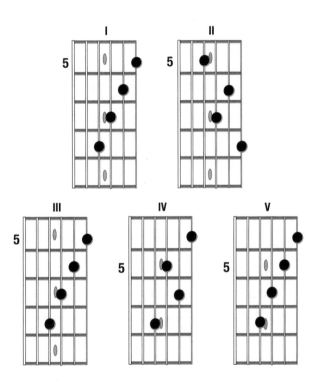

What You Do

Here are three alternating chord shapes that see fingers 1 and 4 and then fingers 2 and 3 swapping strings.

Points To Watch

The fourth finger doesn't much like moving independently of the third and has to be trained to do so if it's going to become fully functional for playing guitar. Even fingers 2 and 3 can be 'sticky' to begin with, so this exercise will probably feel difficult or even impossible if you're still a relative newcomer to the rigours of the instrument. But perseverance is highly recommended!

How It Benefits You

This workout is essential training for the left hand that will pay dividends in both chord changing and general guitar duties. (Note: the exercise comprises changing between I, II, III and IV. Position V is illustrated merely to complete the cycle.)

Standard	Number Of Repeats In Two Minutes
Beginner	10–20
Intermediate	21–50
Advanced	51–70

WORKOUT 28

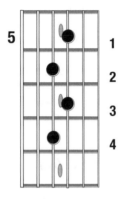

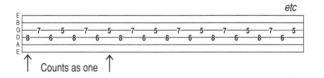

Counts as one

etc

What You Do

This exercise is built around two strings and four notes that can prove to be a real picking conundrum! Position the fingers very carefully for this one, as a moment's lapse of concentration can prove fatal.

Points To Watch

When you're picking between two strings, the temptation is to let the alternate-picking rule slip. Don't! Make sure that your right hand abides by the regulations or things will rapidly fall apart.

How It Benefits You

Both left and right hands take up their individual burdens in this workout. Picking co-ordination and accurate fingering all have to count if this exercise is to work with any fluency.

Standard	Number Of Repeats In Two Minutes
Beginner	10–20
Intermediate	21–50
Advanced	51–100

WORKOUT 29

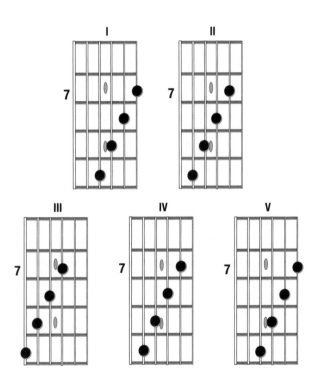

What You Do

Here's a single chord shape repeated across the fretboard in groups of four strings.

Points To Watch

The main thing to here is to keep your fingers in position as you change sets of strings. Make sure that all four left-hand fingers descend onto the fretboard at once. Stragglers will be shot!

How It Benefits You

Accurate chord changing is the name of the game in this workout – and, indeed, one of the mainstays of guitar playing right across the stylistic spectrum. (Note: the exercise comprises changing between positions I, II, III and IV. Position V is illustrated merely to complete the cycle.)

Standard	Number Of Repeats In Two Minutes
Beginner	10–20
Intermediate	21–40
Advanced	41–66

WORKOUT 30

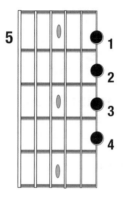

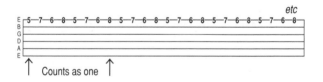

Counts as one

What You Do

This exercise requires you to play a set of four chromatic notes on the top E string, but in a cunning configuration to get those digits dancing!

Points To Watch

Take special note of the fingering. You're operating in a left hand 1-3-2-4 pattern, and don't let this slip as you try to pick up speed. Keep an eye on the right-hand picking, too, and remember to keep it strictly alternate at all times.

How It Benefits You

This workout should enhance and help build your general dexterity with both left and right hands.

Standard	Number Of Repeats In Two Minutes
Beginner	10–15
Intermediate	16–50
Advanced	51–100

WORKOUT 31

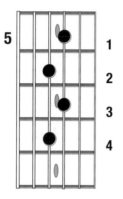

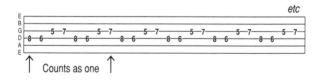

Counts as one

What You Do

This exercise has four notes lying pretty much central on the fingerboard, but a devious left-hand fingering, combined with cross-picking, guarantees a less-than-straightforward morning in the guitar gym!

Points To Watch

A good way of waking up the left hand, this exercise calls for a 4-2-1-3 finger configuration, which will make sure that your brain has managed to find first gear and is sending out valid instructions. Take things slowly at first, make accuracy your goal and keep picking strictly alternate at all times.

How It Benefits You

Any exercise that calls for greater accuracy in both fretting and picking has got to be worthwhile. You'll thank me in the end...

Standard	Number Of Repeats In Two Minutes
Beginner	8–15
Intermediate	16–50
Advanced	51–100

WORKOUT 32

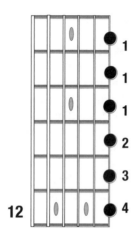

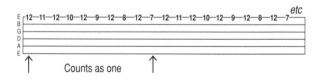

Counts as one

What You Do

This exercise is a game of chase for the first finger on the left hand. Spanning no less than six frets on the top E string, the first finger gets three of them to itself. It's a fairly demanding stretch, too...

Points To Watch

Keep the left hand as much in position as you can. Don't make any extreme side-to-side movements, as this will impair accuracy. The fourth finger comes in for quite a blasting in this workout, too, and if it's still a little weak, you'll have to build speed up slowly. Just remember that speed isn't why we're here. Accuracy rules!

How It Benefits You

Accuracy, co-ordination and picking skills are all brought into line with this workout. A little gentle stretching to increase the effective span of the left hand is another thing taken into account, too.

Standard	Number Of Repeats In Two Minutes
Beginner	5–20
Intermediate	21–45
Advanced	46–100

WORKOUT 33

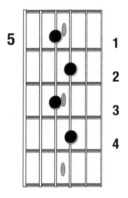

5   1

                     2

                     3

                     4

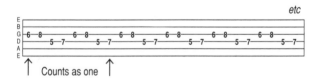

etc

↑ Counts as one ↑

What You Do

Four notes, two strings, contrived fingering. Set your hand in position and take a while to study the fingering. Starting on the second finger might faze you at first, especially if you've already examined some of the other fingerings based on this configuration contained in this section!

Points To Watch

Apart from the left-hand fingering, take care with the right hand's duties, too. Picking two notes on the third string followed by two on the fourth means that your alternate picking skills are going to be put to the test.

How It Benefits You

All left-hand fingers are involved equally in this workout, so the hand is going to warm up nicely after only two minutes. The right hand gets a fair amount of attention, too.

Standard	Number Of Repeats In Two Minutes
Beginner	10–15
Intermediate	16–50
Advanced	51–100

WORKOUT 34

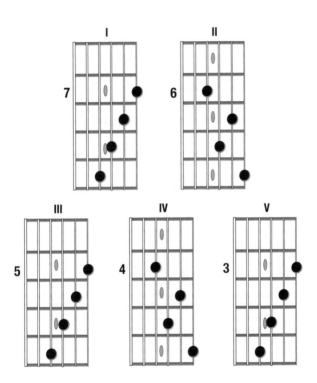

What You Do

Descend the fretboard with these two alternating chord shapes from the seventh fret to the third, gently teasing the left hand's natural four-fret span and general agility.

Points To Watch

Be aware that the left-hand third and fourth fingers don't like moving independently of one another, so changing between shapes in even a single position can represent something of a challenge. Add to this the gradual descent and you've got something very demanding indeed. Take your time and make sure every chord shape is clear and well defined.

How It Benefits You

The art of accurate chord changing is brought into sharp focus with this exercise. The right hand can figuratively put its feet up and relax, here; it doesn't matter whether you pick or pluck, it's the left hand's turn to pump iron!

Standard	Number Of Repeats In Two Minutes
Beginner	8–15
Intermediate	16–30
Advanced	31–60

WORKOUT 35

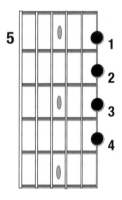

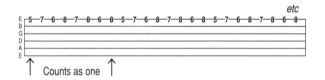

What You Do

This workout combines a four-fret left-hand span with another fingering to test and tease. You can leave the first finger safely anchored while the other fingers carry out their duties. Just make sure you pay the fingering pattern special attention before attempting speed up.

Points To Watch

Don't let the left-hand fingers hover too far from the fretboard when they're not actually in use during this exercise. Try to cut down and streamline at all times the amount of movement that the left hand has to make. After all, the less it has to move, the more efficient it is.

How It Benefits You

Right- and left-hand efficiency is put to the test in this workout. Seeing as this forms the basis for much of what is done on the guitar, you really can't go wrong!

Standard	Number Of Repeats In Two Minutes
Beginner	8–15
Intermediate	16–50
Advanced	51–100

WORKOUT 36

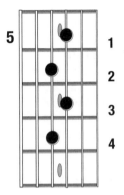

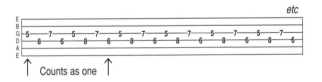

What You Do

This exercise has a series of four notes spread over the D and G strings with a 1-4-3-2 left-hand fingering and right-hand picking over two strings thrown in for good measure, making this an ideal warm-up.

Points To Watch

Be absolutely sure that you've mastered the fingering before beginning to build speed, as mistakes are difficult to correct later on. Watch your picking, as ever, to ensure that it remains strictly alternate at all times.

How It Benefits You

All of the various skills employed in single-note playing on the guitar are brought together in this workout. With luck, the added flexibility this exercise accords you will be a bonus during the rest of your practice routine.

Standard	Number Of Repeats In Two Minutes
Beginner	8–15
Intermediate	16–50
Advanced	51–100

WORKOUT 37

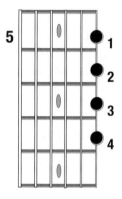

5

1
2
3
4

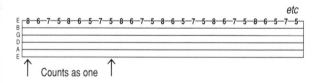

Counts as one

What You Do

This workout covers four frets chromatically on the top
E string, but the fingering for the left hand is anything
but straightforward! Keep your left hand in such a
position that it's in a one-finger-per-fret configuration
and follow the fingering shown in the tab.

Points To Watch

If you like, for this workout you can keep your left-
hand first finger permanently on fret 5, which has the
benefit of anchoring the hand for added stability.
However, some players find that this inhibits movement
and adds confusion, seeing as the exercise begins with
the fourth finger.

How It Benefits You

Single-string picking and left-hand finger agility are
both high on the agenda for this workout.

Standard	Number Of Repeats In Two Minutes
Beginner	8–15
Intermediate	16–60
Advanced	61–100

WORKOUT 38

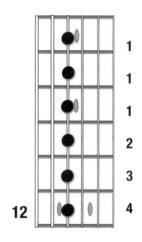

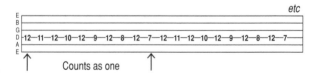

etc

Counts as one

What You Do

Here's a six-fret chromatic chase down the D string, with the left-hand first finger extending its duties to cover three frets. The demands on the fourth finger are quite high, too, as it plays every other note throughout.

Points To Watch

Don't reposition the left hand. Try instead to stretch the first finger back – although, if this causes any discomfort at all, stop immediately! Watch your picking hand, too, to make sure it's following the alternating route and not coming up with some of its own variations.

How It Benefits You

You'll find similar exercises to this one at other points in this section, but not on the D string. Playing similar exercises on different strings, or at different frets, can make a surprising difference, so don't be alarmed if you've been able to perform this workout fluently on the top E string but find some difficulty here.

Standard	Number Of Repeats In Two Minutes
Beginner	10–20
Intermediate	21–60
Advanced	61–110

WORKOUT 39

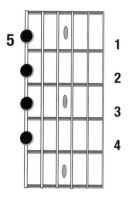

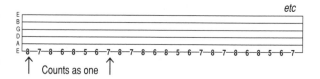

What You Do

This workout is based on four chromatic notes on the bass E string, with the left-hand fourth finger alternating with that hand's other digits. Once you've set up a comfortable hand position, it shouldn't be necessary for either hand or fingers to make too much movement.

Points To Watch

If your left-hand fourth finger isn't yet strong enough, take it easy in the initial stages as its role here is quite demanding. Also, you're operating at the edge of the left hand's reach across the fretboard, and this is likely to raise some orienteering questions at first. Take your time and remember that accuracy is paramount.

How It Benefits You

This kind of exercise is vital for training the left hand to operate anywhere on the neck. It also has the right hand picking in what may be an unfamiliar fashion, in that its duties are confined solely to the bass string.

Standard	Number Of Repeats In Two Minutes
Beginner	8–15
Intermediate	16–60
Advanced	61–100

WORKOUT 40

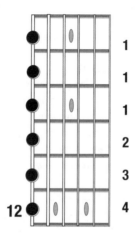

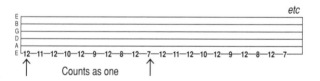

Counts as one

What You Do

Here's game of chromatic tag down the bass E string, with the first and fourth left-hand fingers called upon to perform above and beyond the call of duty!

Points To Watch

Anything you do on the bass E string means that your hand is at the limit of its reach over the neck, which calls for slight adjustments to thumb position and general orientation. Take this into account before trying to increase speed. Make sure that the wrist isn't distorted, as this can quickly lead to RSI (Repetitive Strain Injury) and similar medical conditions. In general, take it easy.

How It Benefits You

Basically, the left-hand fingers should operate with equal efficiency over the entire width of the guitar fretboard, and this workout helps to bring this about.

Standard	Number Of Repeats In Two Minutes
Beginner	10–20
Intermediate	21–60
Advanced	61–100

2 CO-ORDINATION

The principal emphasis in the following exercises is developing accurate position changes, both along and across the guitar fretboard. You'll find yourself hopping from string to string and back again, occasionally spanning as much as 12 frets. This will do wonders for your general accuracy; most guitar parts don't call for this sort of movement on the fretboard, so these workouts should put you in pretty good stead for anything you meet out there in the real world. But that's what the practice room is for, to tease, stretch and generally extend your physical ability and general technique to the point at which you can laugh off just about anything that's thrown at you out there on the bandstand.

Each workout has been designed to test your picking and fretting skills to quite a high degree, and the rules are the same as they were for Chapter 1: aim for extreme accuracy, not sloppy speed. Your two minutes start now...

WORKOUT 1

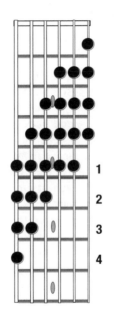

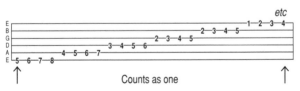

Counts as one

114

What You Do

This exercise involves you playing a chromatic scale from the bass E to the top E string in a sort of semi-diagonal fashion. The left-hand fingering is strictly 1-2-3-4 and several position changes are called for along the way.

Points To Watch

You might have to spend a few moments orienteering before you can see exactly how this workout works. The exercise is based down near the guitar's nut, so the left-hand span is quite full. Make sure that your picking remains alternate throughout the scale – no slip-ups!

How It Benefits You

The chromatic scale is every note used in Western music played in succession, so the benefits here are twofold: your ear is becoming familiar with music's alphabet and your fingers are finding out how to play it – possibly the most useful music resource around.

Standard	Number Of Repeats In Two Minutes
Beginner	1–5
Intermediate	6–20
Advanced	21–40

WORKOUT 2

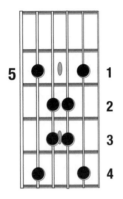

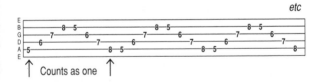

etc

↑ Counts as one ↑

What You Do

Here are two interlaced chord shapes to be played across four strings, backwards and forwards. Work out how the shapes are placed on the neck before you start. Get the left-hand fingering well ingrained before you address the right hand's duties.

Points To Watch

The right hand might have a few nightmares with picking here at first, but in a short while everything should run like clockwork. Make sure that the picking remains alternate.

How It Benefits You

Picking across strings is one of guitar playing's most basic co-ordinated movements. It's essential for accompaniment, in some instances, so this workout will really put you to the test.

Standard	Number Of Repeats In Two Minutes
Beginner	5–15
Intermediate	16–80
Advanced	81–100

WORKOUT 3

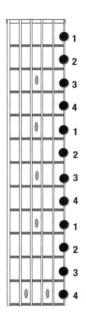

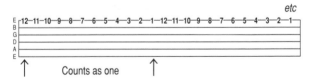

Counts as one

What You Do

This exercise demands three position changes and every note to be played on the top E string from the 12th to the 1st fret – a real test of co-ordination!

Points To Watch

It's the position changes that will slow you down the most here, so take your time to integrate them into the exercise. Play each note with equal duration – don't allow yourself to slow down when the left hand changes position. To someone listening, it should sound like a seamless stream of 12 notes.

How It Benefits You

Swift position changes can cause problems with the flow of some guitar pieces. This workout prepares you for one of the more extreme examples.

Standard	Number Of Repeats In Two Minutes
Beginner	4–10
Intermediate	11–50
Advanced	51–90

WORKOUT 4

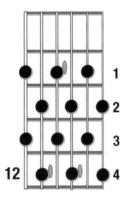

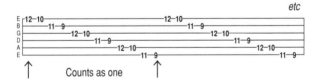

etc

Counts as one

What You Do

Here's a symmetric pattern to be played across all six strings, between frets 9 and 12, with a fingering that alternates between 2 and 4 and between 1 and 3.

Points To Watch

This is a one-way ticket across the guitar neck. At the end of the exercise, you have to reposition your fingers on the top E string to continue. This, combined with the finger-twister that has preceded it, is a real test of picking skills and co-ordinated movement.

How It Benefits You

It's more essential orienteering for both hands. When you begin playing, you have to keep looking at both hands to see where things are. Eventually, you begin to feel your way. This workout sets you on that path.

Standard	Number Of Repeats In Two Minutes
Beginner	5–10
Intermediate	11–40
Advanced	41–60

WORKOUT 5

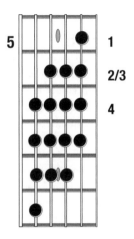

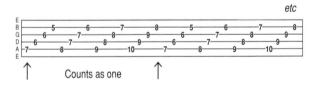

etc

Counts as one

What You Do

It's best to look at the tab for this exercise. Four major-sixth-type chord shapes descend the neck to test your cross-picking and chord-changing skills.

Points To Watch

Once you've sorted out the chord shape, the neck diagram will begin to make more sense. Watch the left-hand fingering and leave your index finger on the second string to act as a guide for the hand. Pick across the strings on each chord, from bass to treble, and try to make each change inaudible to the naked ear.

How It Benefits You

Once again, it's picking across the strings while the left hand's busy changing position that really puts all of your co-ordination skills on red alert.

Standard	Number Of Repeats In Two Minutes
Beginner	5–10
Intermediate	11–30
Advanced	31–48

WORKOUT 6

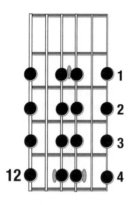

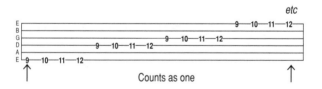

Counts as one

What You Do

Here's a series of sets of four chromatic notes to be played on four strings, bass to treble. The skill here is to position the left and right hands to play each of the sets accurately and seamlessly.

Points To Watch

The problem here might be in knowing which strings to leave out rather than which ones to play! Start slowly and build up speed gradually as you become more confident.

How It Benefits You

Guitar solos or melody passages aren't always positioned neatly so that they run from string to string consecutively. This workout prepares you for missing out strings while still maintaining the necessary accuracy.

Standard	Number Of Repeats In Two Minutes
Beginner	5–10
Intermediate	11–40
Advanced	41–60

WORKOUT 7

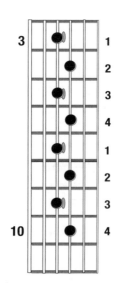

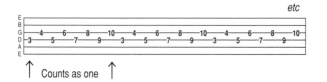

etc

Counts as one

What You Do

This workout has a recurring pattern on two strings over two separate positions – a real co-ordination obstacle course!

Points To Watch

The difficulty here will be in joining the two positions together with no audible gap in between. The position change must run smoothly and sound like a single stream of notes with equal rhythmic value.

How It Benefits You

Position changes are rife in guitar playing and a high degree of accuracy is required before everything gels together. This workout starts you off on the right path.

Standard	Number Of Repeats In Two Minutes
Beginner	8–15
Intermediate	16–40
Advanced	41–60

WORKOUT 8

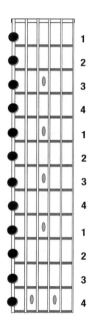

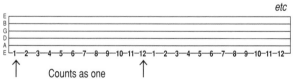

etc

Counts as one

128

What You Do

This exercise requires you to play every note on the bass E string from fret 1 to fret 12, with three position changes along the way to test your mettle!

Points To Watch

Make sure that those position changes remain audibly unnoticed while you play up the bass string. Keep a watchful eye on your right-hand picking, too, as it can really let your fluency down if you allow things to become sloppy.

How It Benefits You

The bass string is awkward to manoeuvre on while you're still finding your way around on the guitar, so this workout should start putting you straight.

Standard	Number Of Repeats In Two Minutes
Beginner	4–10
Intermediate	11–35
Advanced	36–50

WORKOUT 9

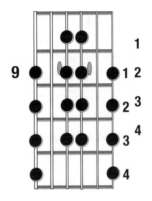

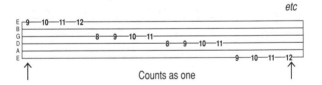

Counts as one

What You Do

With this workout, you have to play four sets of chromatic notes on four strings – and you have to move out of position for the middle two. This is not a drill...

Points To Watch

You're expected to move the hand back a fret to play the notes on the third and fourth strings, and this might cause you trouble. Make a high degree of accuracy your aim here; speed will follow later. Keep an eye on that right-hand picking, too...

How It Benefits You

Picking, position changing and accurate co-ordination all come together in this workout.

Standard	Number Of Repeats In Two Minutes
Beginner	5–10
Intermediate	11–40
Advanced	41–50

WORKOUT 10

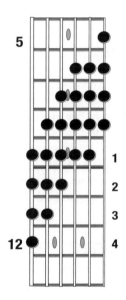

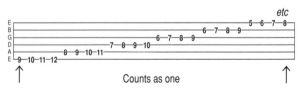

Counts as one

What You Do

Here's a chromatic scale that spans from the 12th fret to the 5th fret, representing a monster challenge for your picking and position-changing skills!

Points To Watch

Managing the picking and position changing is going to give you the most torture, initially. Start very slow and try to aim for something that sounds like a fountain of notes.

How It Benefits You

I can't stress how beneficial it is for your ear to get to hear the chromatic scale at every stage. It's the musical motherlode – and a great test of co-ordination, too.

Standard	Number Of Repeats In Two Minutes
Beginner	2–5
Intermediate	6–20
Advanced	21–40

WORKOUT 11

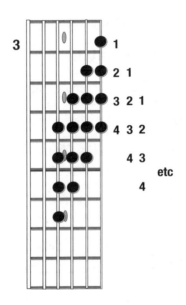

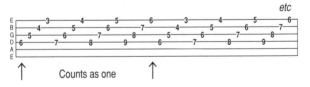

What You Do

Here are four chord shapes to be played arpeggio fashion, ascending the guitar neck chromatically – a real test of your position-changing skills!

Points To Watch

Both hands will probably take a little while to settle into their individual roles in this workout. The picking hand needs to remain scrupulously alternate throughout while the left hand makes those position changes smoothly and rhythmically.

How It Benefits You

Smoothly played arpeggios sound great as an accompaniment to many pieces in the guitar's repertoire and this workout will smoothe those rough edges nicely.

Standard	Number Of Repeats In Two Minutes
Beginner	5–10
Intermediate	11–20
Advanced	21–60

WORKOUT 12

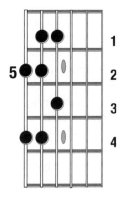

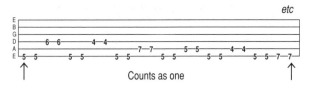

Counts as one

What You Do

This workout comprises an A major scale, with every note double-picked and alternating with the root note at the same time.

Points To Watch

There's a lot of backwards and forwards with the pick in this exercise; sometimes you're playing on adjacent strings, sometimes the same string, sometimes missing one out altogether. Then there's the double-picking to keep up and running, too, so take all of these separate elements and build things up slowly and gradually. Remember, accuracy is paramount!

How It Benefits You

There's an awful lot of musical information being fed into the ear during this exercise, as well as all the technical hanky-panky, so the benefits really are manifold.

Standard	Number Of Repeats In Two Minutes
Beginner	2–5
Intermediate	6–20
Advanced	21–40

WORKOUT 13

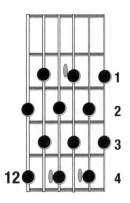

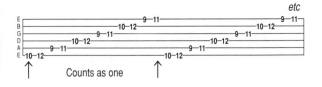

What You Do

Here's a pattern of notes across the fretboard with a 2-and-4/1-and-3 configuration throughout.

Points To Watch

Make sure you've mastered the fingering for this exercise before you attempt to speed it up. When you reach the top E string, don't move the hand to return to the bass string; instead, move the fingers. Finger 2 should be making its way back as soon as finger 3 has finished playing its last note in the series.

How It Benefits You

I see this type of exercise as being similar to making footballers run through tyres during their training. Indeed, the benefits are similar, in terms of sharpening your co-ordination skills. Aim for the first division!

Standard	Number Of Repeats In Two Minutes
Beginner	3–10
Intermediate	11–45
Advanced	46–80

WORKOUT 14

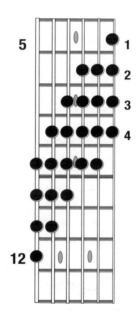

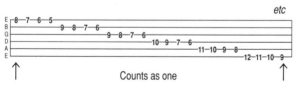

Counts as one

What You Do

This exercise has a descending chromatic scale between the 5th and 12th frets, with an awkward position change in between. Go to red alert!

Points To Watch

The real challenge here is in the fact that the scale is only one way – it doesn't have a return journey that will set the hand up nicely to begin again. Instead, you've got to make quite a considerable move with the left hand to begin each repeat. Begin this exercise dead slow to make sure that all of the variables – picking, etc – are acting together.

How It Benefits You

It's a monster scale with monstrous musical implications, too. Your ear is hearing some very important things while your hands are working at working together.

Standard	Number Of Repeats In Two Minutes
Beginner	2–5
Intermediate	6–20
Advanced	21–40

WORKOUT 15

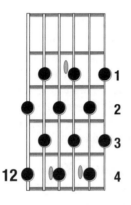

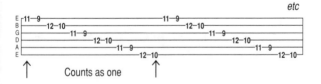

etc

Counts as one

What You Do

This workout will have your fingers running through hoops – literally! It takes the form of a criss-cross pattern on the fingerboard, where the left-hand fingers have to play in an alternating 3-and-1/4-and-2 configuration.

Points To Watch

Once again, make sure that you've really got the fingering well and truly established before bringing this exercise up to speed. There are a lot of elements to balance – picking, fingering and so on have all got to be finely synchronised.

How It Benefits You

Being as sure-footed as possible on the fretboard forms the basis of solid technique for guitarists and this exercise will hone that necessary combination of skills nicely.

Standard	Number Of Repeats In Two Minutes
Beginner	5–10
Intermediate	11–45
Advanced	46–80

WORKOUT 16

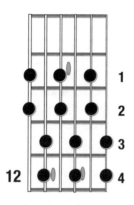

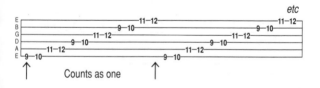

etc

Counts as one

What You Do

This workout has a pattern across the guitar fretboard that alternates between sets of fingers: 1 and 2 followed by 3 and 4.

Points To Watch

Fingers 3 and 4 tend to be considered the weaker recruits in the guitar-playing assault squad, so the fact that you're meant to 'lead' with these two fingers on certain strings might expose a blip in your technique. Take care to ensure that each note has an equal dynamic, as this will call for good co-ordination between the right and left hands.

How It Benefits You

An exercise designed to make the fingers of your left hand more of a team and less of a set of individuals has got to be a good thing!

Standard	Number Of Repeats In Two Minutes
Beginner	5–10
Intermediate	11–45
Advanced	46–80

WORKOUT 17

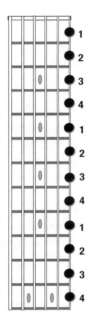

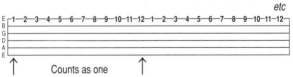

etc

Counts as one

What You Do

Here's a chromatic series covering 12 frets and three hand positions on the top E string – an exercise in seamless note engineering!

Points To Watch

The actual position shifts have to be spot-on accurate or the whole exercise will quickly fall to pieces. Eventually, your hand will know instinctively how far it must move in order to make each position change work, but in the initial stages it has to learn.

How It Benefits You

A combination of skills come together in a beneficial mêlée in this workout. Remember, too, that your brain hearing the chromatic scale time and time again will help your basic understanding of music considerably.

Standard	Number Of Repeats In Two Minutes
Beginner	5–10
Intermediate	11–45
Advanced	46–80

WORKOUT 18

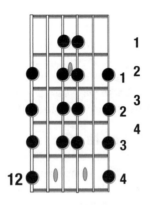

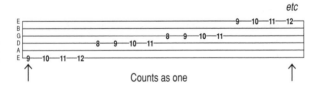

Counts as one

What You Do

This exercise has four groups of chromatic notes set out on four strings, with a slightly nasty position change thrown in for good measure. Man the lifeboats!

Points To Watch

In this workout, take a few moments to orientate your left hand. Make sure that you know where you have to adjust your position and how things are going to work when you get there. Keep your picking under strict alternate control, too.

How It Benefits You

This is a real test of your co-ordination skills, aimed to ensure that you can move across strings and shift position with pinpoint accuracy.

Standard	Number Of Repeats In Two Minutes
Beginner	4–8
Intermediate	9–25
Advanced	26–60

WORKOUT 19

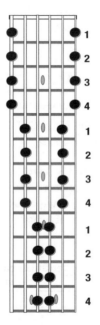

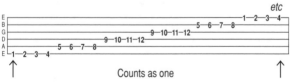

Counts as one

What You Do

Don't panic! This exercise looks a lot more daunting than it really is. Here we have six sets of chromatic note groups spread symmetrically across the fretboard, with some cunning position changes along the way.

Points To Watch

In order to orientate yourself successfully for this workout, you'll need to take things dead slow in the initial stages. The notes won't sound like they belong together, so you've no aural landmarks to guide you – you'll have to rely on developing a good autopilot to get around the many shifts of position occurring here.

How It Benefits You

Well, the guys in the crow's nest are getting twitchy with all these tales of icebergs ahead, but having navigated safely through these waters, you'll laugh in the face of most of the stormy weather music has in store for you!

Standard	Number Of Repeats In Two Minutes
Beginner	2–5
Intermediate	6–20
Advanced	21–40

WORKOUT 20

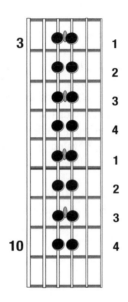

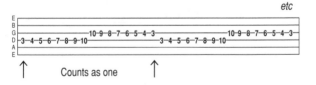

Counts as one

What You Do

For some reason, I think of this workout as being like a game of snakes and ladders. Here, you have to ascend the neck on the D string and then make the return journey on the G string. Oh, and there are some S-bend position changes to cope with, too...

Points To Watch

You're covering a fair amount of ground here, so a few moments' assimilation will be necessary before you get the exercise moving. Aim for everything to sound continuous – someone overhearing you play this shouldn't be able to detect any pauses or even think that you're having to move around.

How It Benefits You

It's a dead basic co-ordination, position-changing, alternate-picking skirmish that will enhance your fluency as a player considerably.

Standard	Number Of Repeats In Two Minutes
Beginner	3–8
Intermediate	9–30
Advanced	31–60

WORKOUT 21

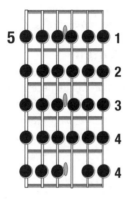

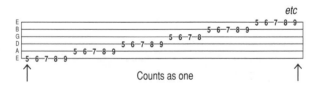

Counts as one

What You Do

Here's an alternative fingering for the chromatic scale
– you might have already met the 'diagonal' version, if
you've been using this book for a while. The trial to
overcome here is the fact that, for most of the time,
you're dealing with four fingers playing over five frets.

Points To Watch

The fourth finger is under pressure to play two notes
per string (except for the G string), and yet everything
has to run as fluently as possible. Try not to move your
left hand while this is happening; instead, merely move
the fourth finger to one side in a gentle stretching motion.

How It Benefits You

Aside from the benefits of hearing the chromatic scale,
this workout really sets you up for position-playing on
the fretboard. You've just come face to face with the
fact that a chromatic scale played in one position covers
five frets – and you've survived!

Standard	Number Of Repeats In Two Minutes
Beginner	1–4
Intermediate	5–15
Advanced	16–33

WORKOUT 22

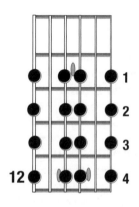

etc

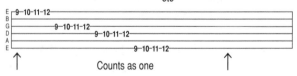

Counts as one

What You Do
Here, you're playing across four of the guitar's six strings, from the top E to the bass E in groups of four.

Points To Watch
Make sure that each note occupies the same rhythmic space – work with a metronome to keep things tight. Pay special attention to the co-ordination between the left and right hands and don't speed up unless everything is spotlessly clean.

How It Benefits You
Practising scales is all well and good, and of course forms an essential part of your musical training, but scales teach you to pick sequentially and so missing a string out here and there comes as quite a shock for both hands. Spend some time here and you'll laugh about it later on.

Standard	Number Of Repeats In Two Minutes
Beginner	4–7
Intermediate	8–25
Advanced	26–60

WORKOUT 23

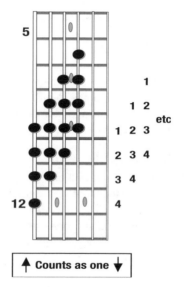

5

1
1 2
etc
1 2 3
2 3 4
3 4
12   4

↑ **Counts as one** ↓

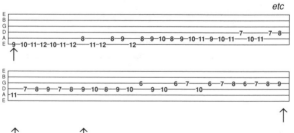

etc

```
E
B
G
D
A
E  9—10—11—12—10—11—12———8———————8—9—————8—9—10—8—9—10—11—9—10—11—————————7———7—8—
                          11—12———12                              10—11———
   ↑
```

```
E
B
G
D  ———————7—8—9—7—8—9—10—8—9—10——————6————6—7————6—7—8—6—7—8—9—
A  11                           9—10———————10———
E
```

↑   ↑   ↑

What You Do

Congratulations! You've landed on the most diabolical workout in the book. This exercise started out as a simple chromatic scale, but instead of picking it sequentially there's a 'picking pattern' involved, just to make sure that an easy life evades you.

Points To Watch

The most important thing in this workout is to understand the pattern. That way, you'll be able to anticipate how the whole thing sounds, which will make everything a lot easier. All the same, it still means that finger 1 is going to be stretched continually as the scales meanders sideways.

How It Benefits You

An exercise like this stretches your technique on almost every level – picking, fingering, position changing...you name it, it's all here. Don't have nightmares!

Standard	Number Of Repeats In Two Minutes
Beginner	1–3
Intermediate	4–10
Advanced	11–18

WORKOUT 24

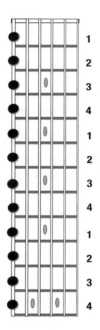

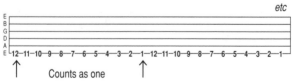

Counts as one

etc

What You Do

More chromatic gymnastics with a descending scale on the bass E string, complete with position shifts in abundance.

Points To Watch

Your brain has to act like air-traffic control when co-ordinating this sort of exercise. Keeping control of your alternate picking and position-shifting while ensuring everything remains even and well tempered – rhythmically speaking – could cause a few near misses at first, so proceed slowly, buckle up and please make sure that your tray is in an upright position.

How It Benefits You

You won't find position shifts quite so radical out there in the real world, but command of the fretboard is everything and this workout pushes your skills in this area to the limits.

Standard	Number Of Repeats In Two Minutes
Beginner	5–10
Intermediate	11–45
Advanced	46–80

WORKOUT 25

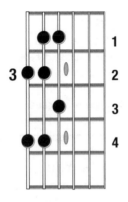

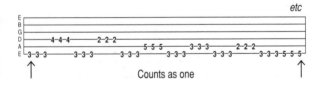

Counts as one

What You Do

This one has you triple-picking over a descending G major scale, with the scale's root played every other note.

Points To Watch

This is one instance where strict alternate picking needn't be adhered to. Each note in this exercise is a triplet – one beat split evenly into three. To count a triplet, either say a three-syllable word on every beat ('evenly' is a good one) or count '1-2-3, 1-2-3, 1-2-3', etc. When you pick a triplet, it's best to use a downstroke at the start of every beat, so your picking regime would be 'down-up-down, down-up-down, down-up-down', and so on. This is bound to cause the odd glitch here and there, especially as your alternate picking is probably now a well-oiled machine...

How It Benefits You

Your ear is hearing a scale; your right hand has got something radical to come to terms with; the left hand, meanwhile, merely plays a scale. Be brave.

Standard	Number Of Repeats In Two Minutes
Beginner	1–3
Intermediate	4–11
Advanced	12–26

WORKOUT 26

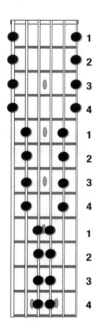

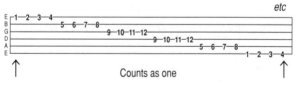

Counts as one

What You Do

This exercise is built around an ascent and descent of the guitar neck, with some string changing along the way. Not the easiest way to traverse the fretboard, perhaps; just think of it as the scenic route!

Points To Watch

Make sure that both hands and head know what's meant to be going on in this workout, as mistakes could be costly, once things are up and running. Keep a check on the picking, too – see that it's strictly alternate at all times and aim for 100 per cent smooth accuracy.

How It Benefits You

You don't have to dart around the neck this often usually, but that's what practising is for. If you're fully prepared for an event such as this one, you're sure to be able to deal with most things that you come across in practical terms.

Standard	Number Of Repeats In Two Minutes
Beginner	2–5
Intermediate	6–20
Advanced	21–40

WORKOUT 27

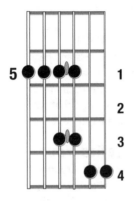

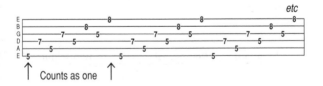

etc

Counts as one

What You Do

Here's a series of octaves played over all six strings with a picking strategy that could slow things down a lot.

Points To Watch

Take extreme care with the picking here. Think of it like a mathematical series – you're picking strings 6, 4, 5, 3, 4, 2, 3, 1 each time, and this could cause some initial orienteering problems. The telltale sign that something's amiss and that an error has crept in somewhere would be that the exercise starts to sound very unmusical indeed.

How It Benefits You

For the ear, an octave is as valuable an interval with which to be associated as any of the others, and yet it's often not included in ear-training exercises. So, apart from all the frenzied picking going on, the ear is drawing some benefit from this workout, too!

Standard	Number Of Repeats In Two Minutes
Beginner	7–15
Intermediate	16–30
Advanced	31–60

WORKOUT 28

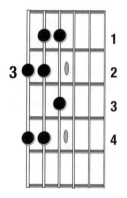

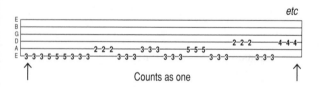

Counts as one

What You Do

On the face of it, this is a G major scale, but the picking orientation sees to it that things are far from being straightforward.

Points To Watch

This exercise should be picked in triplets – literally beats that have been divided into three equal parts. So, for this exercise, you can abandon temporarily your alternate picking regime, because triplets are best played with a downstroke at the start of each beat, so think 'down-up-down' on every group of three. Count '1-2-3, 1-2-3, 1-2-3' to ensure that each is split properly.

How It Benefits You

Your ear is hearing a major scale, which is always a good thing, but everything else – in terms of picking and co-ordination – is being put to the test as well, making this workout a real all-rounder.

Standard	Number Of Repeats In Two Minutes
Beginner	1–4
Intermediate	5–15
Advanced	16–27

WORKOUT 29

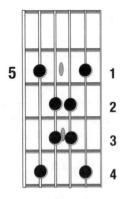

5 · · 1
· · 2
· · 3
· · 4

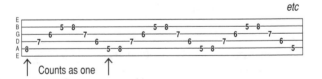

etc

Counts as one

What You Do

In this workout, two chord shapes converge to provide a real test of your arpeggio-playing skills.

Points To Watch

Take a look at the tab and make sure that both of the diagonal chord shapes are well established in your mind before you begin to work. Keep the right hand picking strictly alternate and aim for smooth evenness throughout. Try to economise the movement in your left hand, as any extreme movements will slow things down considerably.

How It Benefits You

Arpeggiated chords are always effective beneath certain ballads, and yet a few guitarists find themselves really out at sea when faced with them for the first time. Here's your chance to be a least one step ahead in the game!

Standard	Number Of Repeats In Two Minutes
Beginner	7–15
Intermediate	16–30
Advanced	31–60

WORKOUT 30

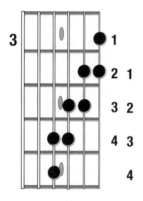

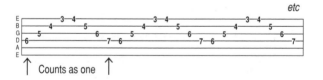

What You Do

Here, two chord shapes and one position shift test your arpeggio playing as well as your position shifting.

Points To Watch

Both of these shapes are quite far down the neck, so your hand will be practically at full stretch, especially if you're still on the lower rungs of the guitar-playing ladder. Use the tab to work out exactly what's required and start things slowly until you're sure of your ground, then speed things up gradually.

How It Benefits You

Cross-picking, combined with a position shift, will put pressure on quite a few areas of your guitar-playing technique here. This sort of exercise prepares a lot of ground for later work, so make sure you dig those foundations deep!

Standard	Number Of Repeats In Two Minutes
Beginner	7–15
Intermediate	16–30
Advanced	31–60

WORKOUT 31

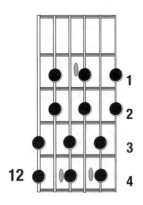

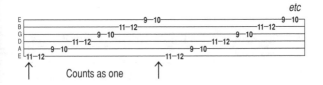

What You Do

This workout calls for considerable finger cunning, as it crosses the strings with a slightly untoward and unpredictable demeanour.

Points To Watch

You're beginning this exercise with fingers 3 and 4 and alternating them with fingers 1 and 2 throughout. Pay special attention to the general flow of the exercise and try to ensure that everything fits together rhythmically. Remember, accuracy comes above speed at all times; speeding up something that is still rhythmically inaccurate is just playing mistakes, only faster.

How It Benefits You

Your general dexterity is being put to the test with this workout. Combining the necessary picking with a tricky left-hand fingering will do wonders for your general playing abilities. Things are going to seem much simpler after a while spent on this beauty!

Standard	Number Of Repeats In Two Minutes
Beginner	5–10
Intermediate	11–40
Advanced	41–80

WORKOUT 32

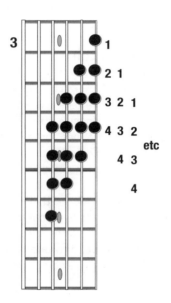

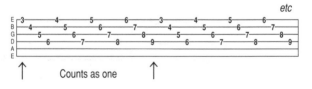

Counts as one

What You Do

Four ascending chord shapes take you further towards arpeggio heaven, though some serious cross-picking and a few position changes may feel more like hell at first!

Points To Watch

In actual fact, this isn't a bad-sounding workout. Exercises are renowned for sounding bad, even while they're doing you good. In any case, pay special attention to your picking; it might feel easier to break the alternate-picking rules here, but it's excellent discipline not to. After all, you didn't think things would be easy down here in guitar boot camp, did you? Keep those position shifts as smooth as possible, too. Eliminate any sloppy tendencies now and you'll reap the rich rewards of your efforts later on.

How It Benefits You

This exercise puts a lot of pressure on you to fine-tune playing elements like cross-picking and prepares the way for developing a professional-sounding accompaniment.

Standard	Number Of Repeats In Two Minutes
Beginner	4–8
Intermediate	9–25
Advanced	26–50

WORKOUT 33

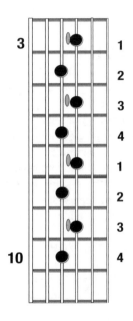

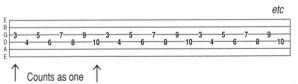

etc

↑ Counts as one ↑

What You Do

Here, picking consecutive notes between two strings, plus a position shift along the way, means that your powers of co-ordination are being tested to the fullest.

Points To Watch

Balancing all of the various elements of this exercise together is a little like spinning plates – let one thing slip and everything falls apart. At first, it's most likely to be the position shift from the third to the seventh fret that confounds you. Take your time and speed things up only when you're absolutely sure that everything is smooth and rhythmic.

How It Benefits You

Cross-picking and relocating your hand on the neck is a guitar-playing staple – it happens all the time. Here, you're digging the foundations of solid technique.

Standard	Number Of Repeats In Two Minutes
Beginner	7–15
Intermediate	16–35
Advanced	36–65

WORKOUT 34

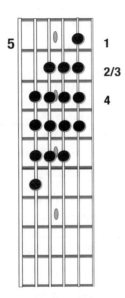

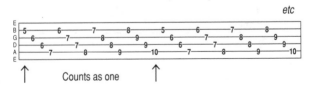

etc

Counts as one

What You Do

Here are some ascending major-sixth chords to arpeggiate up the neck – a cross-picking *tour de force* to test your alternate picking!

Points To Watch

The temptation here is to form the chord shape once and simply move it up the neck in gradual stages. I would actually advise against this. By all means keep your first left-hand finger in place to act as a guide, but reposition all of the other fingers afresh each time. This will ensure that all notes ring for equal value and gives you greater control. In comparison, a chord that is merely slid up the neck sounds sloppy and inarticulate.

How It Benefits You

Picking skills are put to the test in this workout – plus, if you take the advice above, a lesson in dynamics.

Standard	Number Of Repeats In Two Minutes
Beginner	3–8
Intermediate	9–25
Advanced	26–60

WORKOUT 35

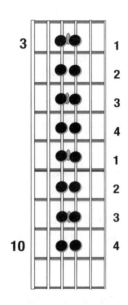

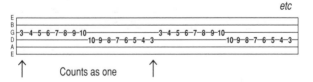

Counts as one

What You Do
It's a case of 'up on the G and down on the D' for this workout, a little chromatic madness to hone those picking skills still further.

Points To Watch
Any exercise that calls for a position shift mid-passage calls for special attention to be paid to general fluency and evenness of performance. If played properly, this workout shouldn't sound as if it's in four separate sections; it should sound like one fluid stream of notes with no fractures on the surface. Take care with picking and only increase speed when things are running together nicely.

How It Benefits You
You're learning far more than how to string blocks of chromatic notes together; there are performance techniques being developed here that will help form the solid backbone of your playing.

Standard	Number Of Repeats In Two Minutes
Beginner	4–8
Intermediate	9–30
Advanced	31–60

WORKOUT 36

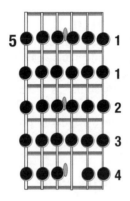

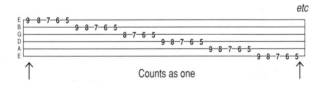

Counts as one

What You Do

Here's a descending chromatic scale where the left-hand first finger gets a lot more than it bargained for!

Points To Watch

This is a chromatic scale covering five frets, so the left-hand first finger has to do more than its fair share. Rather than move the whole hand out of position all the time to play the 'extra' note, it's better for you to stretch the first finger sideways. On the G, however, it's better to change position and adopt a more straightforward 4-3-2-1 fingering. Watch your picking to make sure each note is picked cleanly and in a strict alternating sequence.

How It Benefits You

Again, playing the chromatic scale is hugely beneficial. Add the challenge of shifting positions and accommodating five notes per string (on all except the G) and you have one exercise that can achieve so much. (Note: the fingering for string 3 should be 4-3-2-1.)

Standard	Number Of Repeats In Two Minutes
Beginner	1–4
Intermediate	5–15
Advanced	16–30

WORKOUT 37

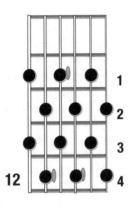

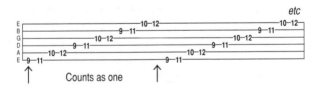

Counts as one

What You Do

It might look like a pretty pattern in the fretboard diagram, but this workout will have you sleeping with the light on for weeks!

Points To Watch

Sort out the left-hand fingering in advance, here. The right hand can content itself with playing two notes per string – nothing too controversial there – but it's the left hand that really needs watching. You're operating with a configuration that goes 1-3, 2-4 across the fretboard. It's not as easy as it sounds, either, especially if the left-hand fourth finger is not yet fully up to speed with the rest of its compatriots.

How It Benefits You

Left-hand finger co-ordination – the mainstay of dealing with just about everything you play on the guitar – is brought into sharp focus in this workout.

Standard	Number Of Repeats In Two Minutes
Beginner	5–10
Intermediate	11–25
Advanced	26–40

WORKOUT 38

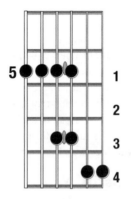

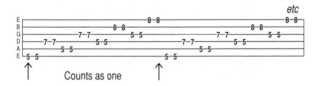

Counts as one

What You Do

This workout calls for some double-picked octaves across the breadth of the fretboard. It's a co-ordination conundrum, too – sometimes you miss a string, sometimes not!

Points To Watch

Somehow, when you're picking every note twice, things can very easily go completely haywire at the drop of a hat. Make sure that the left hand knows where it's got to go first – play everything through dead slow, if need be, then look at getting all pick strokes as even as possible. Aim for a single dynamic across the board and the exercise will sound smooth and streamlined.

How It Benefits You

You're hearing octaves and double-picking across a slightly less than straightforward series of notes, so you can be sure that quite a few areas of technique are being addressed here!

Standard	Number Of Repeats In Two Minutes
Beginner	4–8
Intermediate	9–20
Advanced	21–40

WORKOUT 39

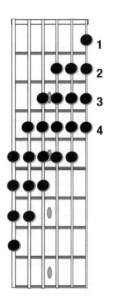

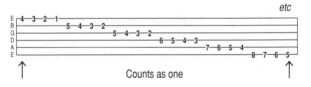

etc

Counts as one

What You Do

Here's a descending 'diagonal' chromatic scale at the end of the guitar fretboard, and yet it travels up the neck.

Points To Watch

Of the two main fingerings for the chromatic scale, this one is probably the more logical, and certainly easier on the left hand! But, in order to get this fingering up and running, you first have to come to terms with several position changes – and the slightly disquieting fact that you seem to be travelling 'up' the fretboard with a series of notes that is obviously descending in pitch. Ignoring that, though, keep an eye on your picking and make sure that you're following the left-hand fingering and tab to the letter.

How It Benefits You

Basic orienteering and picking skills and left-hand finger co-ordination at an optimum level combine in this exercise.

Standard	Number Of Repeats In Two Minutes
Beginner	1–5
Intermediate	6–21
Advanced	22–40

WORKOUT 40

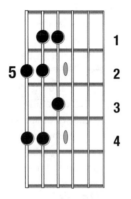

Counts as one

What You Do

Here, you're double-picking each note of an A major scale – alternating every note with the root on the fifth string.

Points To Watch

If you're familiar with basic scale patterns like this one, double-picking might pose a surprising challenge. The fingers instinctively want to follow the path they're most familiar with, and so here's a case when familiarity really can trip you up! You don't go out onstage and play scale shapes, so this kind of exercise will process the same sort of melodic information for you but add the twist of an unfamiliar picking package. Make sure all of those double-picked notes are even – check yourself with a metronome and find out how accurate you really are.

How It Benefits You

Breaking formed habits but still dealing wholesale with vital musical information is pure gold dust for all areas of your development.

Standard	Number Of Repeats In Two Minutes
Beginner	2–5
Intermediate	6–25
Advanced	26–40

3 EAR TRAINING

The workouts in this chapter are primarily concerned with supporting and developing your skills in the often overlooked art of ear training. Everybody knows that rudimentary physical skills such as picking and chord changing have to be worked at before the rewards show up in your playing, but concentrating entirely on these areas alone can leave the musical side of your playing personality under-nourished – and it's no good developing your technical skills to the point that you can pick with surgical accuracy but have nothing directing and moulding your playing musically from within. In fact, if I was about to get dramatic about all this, I'd say that this section could go a long way towards helping you develop something of a musical soul!

A few of the exercises demand that you sing the missing note from a scale or arpeggio, but you're not learning to sing. (I'll leave developing your lead-vocalist skills to you.) Instead, you're equipping yourself with the basic tools of musical awareness, by forging a link between what's happening on your fretboard and what's going on in your head.

You'll find the direction 'Try humming along with this exercise as you play it' turning up quite often in this section. Even if you think that your singing abilities are diabolical, I'd still encourage you to have a go. It's highly important that what you play comes from within you, and this little inner musical voice needs finding and cultivating!

WORKOUT 1

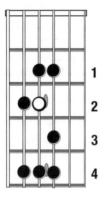

Counts as one

What You Do

Sing the missing note! This is a scale of C major with one of its notes whited out on the fretboard diagram. First, play the scale and listen to the note in question. The next time you play through it, miss out the note on the fretboard and try to sing the correct pitch in its place.

Points To Watch

The missing note here is F, the fourth note of the C major scale – in other words, the interval is a fourth. Try to sing it, then play the note to see how close you were.

How It Benefits You

A focused sense of musical awareness is one of the most crucial tools you'll ever develop. You need to forge a link between what's going on down there on the fretboard and what's happening inside your head. This exercise is a very important first step.

Standard	Number Of Repeats In Two Minutes
Beginner	9–20
Intermediate	21–40
Advanced	41–60

WORKOUT 2

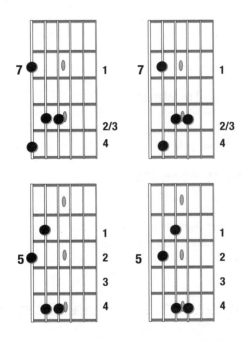

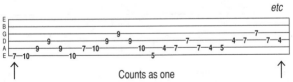

etc

Counts as one

What You Do

This workout comprises four single-octave arpeggios –
two minor and two major – in two positions. Once you're
familiar with the sound of this exercise, try humming
or singing along. It will do your ear a lot of good!

Points To Watch

Watch the left-hand fingering here. On the second pair
of arpeggios, you can play the final two notes with either
finger 4 or fingers 3 and 4. Position-shifting could pose
a few problems, too, so take things dead slow to begin
with. Remember, you're feeding musical information into
your brain, so there's no need to rush things.

How It Benefits You

Realising the difference between major and minor
chords or arpeggios is one of the most fundamental
ear-training skills that you need to acquire. This exercise
should prepare the ground nicely.

Standard	Number Of Repeats In Two Minutes
Beginner	1–5
Intermediate	6–20
Advanced	21–35

WORKOUT 3

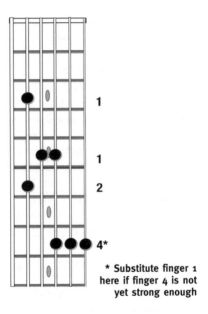

1

1

2

4*

*** Substitute finger 1
here if finger 4 is not
yet strong enough**

Counts as one

What You Do

Here's a two-octave C minor arpeggio with a tricky position shift and a couple of fingering variations.

Points To Watch

The thing to watch here is the fingering in the left hand. The diagram calls for the hand to move right after playing the first note, so that finger 2 is ready to play the second note. Also, the diagram shows finger 4 playing three notes at the end – not possible for an under-developed digit in the early stages of learning. Substituting finger 1 will make things easier but will mean another position shift. Of course, this is only one of a number of fingering variations available. You should try to find the most manageable for you.

How It Benefits You

This is a good technical exercise, but the benefits of letting your ear hear a minor arpeggio repeated a number of times is extremely valuable, too.

Standard	Number Of Repeats In Two Minutes
Beginner	1–3
Intermediate	4–15
Advanced	16–25

WORKOUT 4

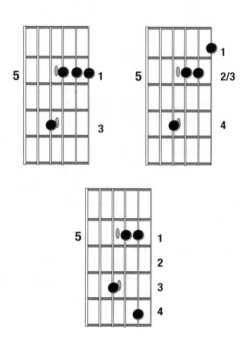

Counts as one

What You Do

Here are three different A minor arpeggios, each of which has a place in the musical repertoire. The first is a straightforward A minor, the second an A minor (major) seventh, the third an A minor seventh. The chord progression upon which these arpeggios are based has been used by everyone from Bach to The Beatles!

Points To Watch

On a technical level, the fingering should be looked at closely, especially the shift between the first and second shapes. Aim for fluidity in the changes so that the exercise sounds like one single stream of notes.

How It Benefits You

The musical information here for your ear to process is of great benefit. It's quite a common musical device and should teach you to differentiate between the various types of minor arpeggio nicely.

Standard	Number Of Repeats In Two Minutes
Beginner	2–6
Intermediate	7–20
Advanced	21–40

WORKOUT 5

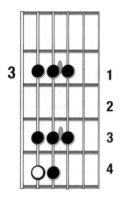

Counts as one

What You Do

Sing the missing note! This is a scale of C minor with one of its notes whited out on the fretboard diagram. First, play the scale and listen to the note in question. The next time you play through it, miss out the note on the fretboard and try to sing the correct pitch in its place.

Points To Watch

The missing note here is the minor third, the single most important note in the scale, as it determines whether the chord is a major or a minor. Take some time to listen to the note by playing it several times before attempting to sing it in place.

How It Benefits You

Music has two genders, major and minor. Drawing your ear's attention to the positioning of the minor third in this way provides you with a vital tool in this respect.

Standard	Number Of Repeats In Two Minutes
Beginner	3–8
Intermediate	9–25
Advanced	26–50

WORKOUT 6

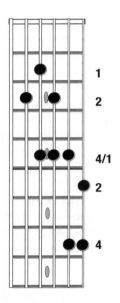

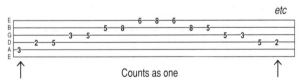

etc

Counts as one

What You Do

Here's a two-octave C7 arpeggio over two positions. Humming or singing along in some fashion is highly recommended for this workout!

Points To Watch

As with nearly all two-octave arpeggios requiring a position change halfway through, fingering becomes something of an issue here. The fingering shown in the diagram recommends that you change position after the second finger has played the fourth note. Persevere with this, as it really is the most logical way of playing through this exercise.

How It Benefits You

The 'sevenths' are the third family of chords, the other two being major and minor, so anything that draws the ear to their distinct tonalities is vital.

Standard	Number Of Repeats In Two Minutes
Beginner	3–8
Intermediate	9–25
Advanced	26–55

WORKOUT 7

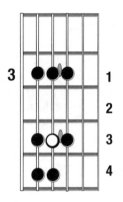

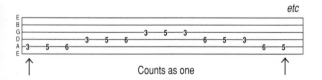

Counts as one

What You Do

Sing the missing note! This is a scale of C minor with one of its notes whited out on the fretboard diagram. First, play the scale and listen to the note in question. The next time you play through it, miss out the note on the fretboard and try to sing the correct pitch in its place.

Points To Watch

The missing note here is the fifth note in the scale. Play through the scale a few times, paying special attention to the position and sound of the fifth, then try to pitch it in position. There are no fingering issues here – in fact, the second finger has earned itself some time off!

How It Benefits You

The fifth is an important member of the scale, as it's also a chord tone, so becoming aware of its relationship with the rest of the minor scale is very valuable indeed.

Standard	Number Of Repeats In Two Minutes
Beginner	3–8
Intermediate	9–25
Advanced	26–50

WORKOUT 8

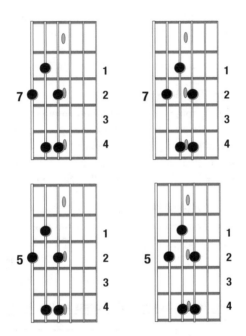

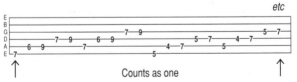

Counts as one

What You Do

Here are four dominant-seventh arpeggios with a position change in the middle, just to liven things up!

Points To Watch

The fingering for all four of these arpeggios should be identical, so it should be a question of merely transferring it to four different places on the fretboard. Make sure that the position changes are inaudible and that the exercise flows like a single stream of notes.

How It Benefits You

Dominant-seventh arpeggios played in this particular configuration have implications beyond the scope of this book (it's known as the cycle of fourths, if you want to look it up somewhere), and so introducing yourself to them at an early stage of musical development is an exceedingly good route to take.

Standard	Number Of Repeats In Two Minutes
Beginner	2–6
Intermediate	7–25
Advanced	26–40

WORKOUT 9

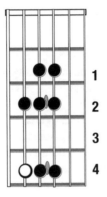

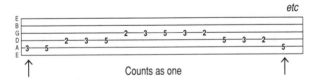

Counts as one

What You Do

Sing the missing note! This is a scale of C dominant seventh with one of its notes whited out on the fretboard diagram. First, play the scale and listen to the note in question. The next time you play through it, miss out the note and try to sing the correct pitch in its place.

Points To Watch

The missing note here is the second member of the dominant scale. Despite the fact that it falls so soon after the root note, the second can be a very difficult note to pitch correctly. Fingering is straightforward – this time, the third finger takes a rest while the rest work up a sweat!

How It Benefits You

Basic, ear-based orienteering with the dominant scale – one of the most important and most often used scales in music – is absolutely vital to ensure your progress, musically. It doesn't matter if you can't sing, either; it's the awareness factor that's so important here.

Standard	Number Of Repeats In Two Minutes
Beginner	2–8
Intermediate	9–25
Advanced	26–40

WORKOUT 10

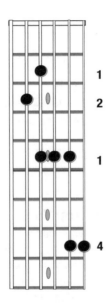

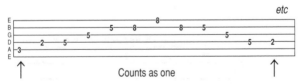

Counts as one

What You Do

This workout has you playing a two-octave C major arpeggio with a position shift in the middle.

Points To Watch

As far as left-hand fingering is concerned, it's best to move your hand immediately after playing the second note of the series. This will line up fingers 1 and 4 to complete the arpeggio. Playing two notes with your fourth finger may pose a few problems; it's best to cover both notes with finger 4 at once and look at it as laying a partial barre. If this isn't possible at first, play each note individually with finger 4. This will slow you up a bit, but you can tell yourself that finger 4 will be strong enough to carry out this important manoeuvre one day!

How It Benefits You

Fact: there are more major chords played in popular music than any other, so familiarising yourself with the sound of them is a priceless skill to have under your belt.

Standard	Number Of Repeats In Two Minutes
Beginner	5–10
Intermediate	11–25
Advanced	26–40

WORKOUT 11

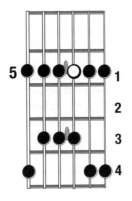

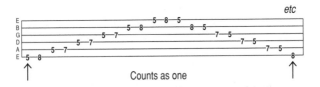

Counts as one

What You Do

Sing the missing note! This an A minor pentatonic scale with one of its notes whited out on the fretboard diagram. First, play the scale and listen to the missing note. The next time you play through it, miss out the note on the fretboard and try to sing the correct pitch.

Points To Watch

The note in question here is the minor third, one of the most important notes in the scale. The minor pentatonic is used principally in blues-orientated rock, and a great amount of its power is derived from the third – known as the 'blue note' when bent slightly sharp. There are no fingering irregularities here and nothing for the second finger to do, either. This is pure ear training.

How It Benefits You

The minor pentatonic scale is very important in modern pop, blues and rock music. Spending even just two minutes with it in the pursuit of ear training is essential.

Standard	Number Of Repeats In Two Minutes
Beginner	2–6
Intermediate	7–25
Advanced	26–40

WORKOUT 12

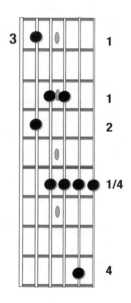

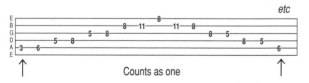

Counts as one

What You Do

This workout has a C minor arpeggio strung over two octaves, calling for two position changes and some slightly less-than-straightforward fingering.

Points To Watch

Spend some time orientating yourself before trying to run with this workout. Moving your left hand immediately after playing the first note will position your second finger so that it's ready to play the second note. The hand has to move once again to facilitate playing the last four notes.

How It Benefits You

Despite the physical challenge that comes with this workout, hearing the minor-seventh arpeggio is good for the ear, as this chord crops up time and time again in blues, jazz and pop music.

Standard	Number Of Repeats In Two Minutes
Beginner	2–7
Intermediate	8–30
Advanced	31–50

WORKOUT 13

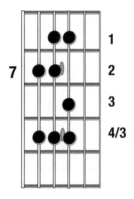

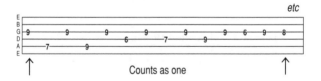

Counts as one

What You Do
This workout has an E major scale with a repeating top note – another picking conundrum!

Points To Watch
Technically, this is known as *pedal point*, meaning a melodic passage with a repetitive upper or lower note. Here, it's reduced to an exercise in order to display each note of the scale's relationship to its upper root. It will take a while for you to become familiar with the fingering – and, for that matter, the right-hand picking – so make sure that you know exactly what's going on before attempting to speed things up. Patience!

How It Benefits You
This is another way of dissecting the major scale – music's most important scale, remember – so that its inner workings are more readily displayed for the ear.

Standard	Number Of Repeats In Two Minutes
Beginner	3–8
Intermediate	9–28
Advanced	29–50

WORKOUT 14

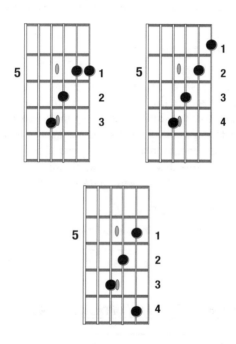

Counts as one

What You Do

Here, three arpeggios demonstrate the difference between a major and a dominant seventh. In order, they are the major, major seventh and dominant seventh.

Points To Watch

This workout is mainly for the ear, but it does present a fingering issue. The hand has to move out of position to play the second arpeggio (a major seventh) before returning to play the third (a dominant seventh). There's also some cross-picking for the right hand to consider, in that things should remain strictly alternate. The focus might be on ear training, but there's no excuse for sloppiness!

How It Benefits You

One common question with music is 'What's the difference between a dominant and a major seventh?' This workout points out the answer: they sound very different to each other and so shouldn't be confused.

Standard	Number Of Repeats In Two Minutes
Beginner	2–7
Intermediate	8–25
Advanced	26–40

WORKOUT 15

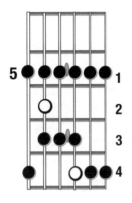

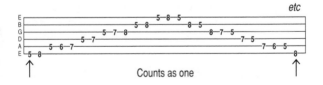

Counts as one

What You Do

Sing the missing notes! This is a scale of A minor pentatonic with two of its notes whited out on the fretboard diagram. First, play the scale and listen to the notes in question. The next time you play through it, miss out the notes on the fretboard and try to sing the correct pitches in their place.

Points To Watch

This represents a real challenge for the ear because the missing notes are both the flat fifth (ie the same note an octave apart). The flat fifth is the note that begins to point the minor-pentatonic scale firmly towards the blues – and it's very difficult to pitch, as you'll find out...

How It Benefits You

The flat fifth lies exactly halfway along the chromatic scale and is the king of dissonance, and yet it's an essential element in all blues-based music. Introducing the ear to its position in the scale is absolutely priceless.

Standard	Number Of Repeats In Two Minutes
Beginner	2–5
Intermediate	6–20
Advanced	21–35

WORKOUT 16

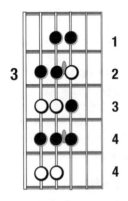

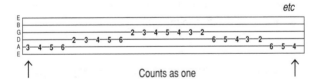

etc

Counts as one

What You Do

Lots of missing notes to sing here! Here is a major scale (the dark blobs) within a chromatic. By singing the white notes, you can hear one being transformed into the other.

Points To Watch

The left-hand fingering asks that you play five frets with four fingers – but only while you're introducing your ears to the notes you're supposed to sing! When you can fill in the notes vocally with confidence, you can return to the simpler major-scale fingering. There are a lot of notes to insert, and hence a lot of notes for the ear to familiarise itself with, but if you try relating the 'missing' notes to the notes on either side, the job is made easier.

How It Benefits You

This exercise will enhance your familiarity with chromatic tones (ie those not naturally members of any particular scale – in this instance, the notes whited out). These notes are often used in blues and jazz to add dissonance.

Standard	Number Of Repeats In Two Minutes
Beginner	1–5
Intermediate	6–25
Advanced	26–40

WORKOUT 17

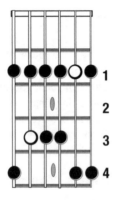

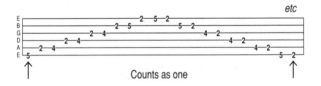

etc

Counts as one

What You Do

Sing the missing notes! This is the A major pentatonic scale with two of its notes whited out on the fretboard diagram. First, play the scale and listen to the notes in question. The next time you play through it, miss out the notes on the fretboard and try to sing the correct pitches in their place.

Points To Watch

The missing note here is the third in the scale of A major. The A major pentatonic is used in blues, country, jazz and pop, and is therefore an important scale to take on board, aurally. There are no fingering concerns for the left hand here – finger 2 gets another day off, in fact. Keep the picking strictly alternate, though.

How It Benefits You

This is a very common scale with one of its more important members missed out for you to vocalise, which will do wonders for that inner musical voice.

Standard	Number Of Repeats In Two Minutes
Beginner	2–6
Intermediate	7–25
Advanced	26–40

WORKOUT 18

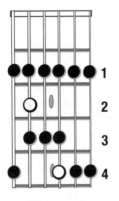

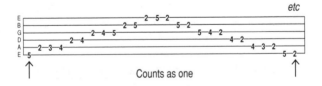

Counts as one

What You Do

Sing the missing notes! This is the A major pentatonic scale with two of its notes whited out. First, play the scale and listen to the notes in question. The next time you play through it, miss out the notes on the fretboard and try to sing the correct pitches in their place.

Points To Watch

Here you have to vocally insert the minor third, which, despite this being a major-type scale, is a powerful note and useful in many different music forms. Just as the blues sometimes sees a major third within minor scales, the opposite can happen, too. Familiarise yourself with the missing note and insert it seamlessly into the scale.

How It Benefits You

In this type of pentatonic scale, the minor third is a powerful *passing note* – that is, a note that connects two or more others during a melodic passage or a solo. This exercise is one way of really getting to know it.

Standard	Number Of Repeats In Two Minutes
Beginner	2–6
Intermediate	7–25
Advanced	26–40

WORKOUT 19

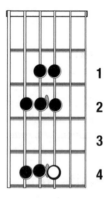

Counts as one

What You Do

Sing the missing note! This is the C dominant-seventh scale with one of its notes whited out on the diagram. First, play the scale and listen to the note in question. The next time you play through it, miss out the note on the fretboard and try to sing the correct pitch in its place.

Points To Watch

This might come as something of a surprise, because the missing note is in fact the root note pitched an octave higher than where you start playing it. But, because this is a dominant scale and so has a tendency to sound 'unfinished', it's an important note to be able to pitch. Quite often, it's the gap between the seventh and eighth notes of this scale that comes as a shock to people who are otherwise unfamiliar with it. Get to know it now!

How It Benefits You

Dominant scales crop up all the time in rock, blues and jazz, so knowing what this note sounds like is vital.

Standard	Number Of Repeats In Two Minutes
Beginner	4–9
Intermediate	10–30
Advanced	31–55

WORKOUT 20

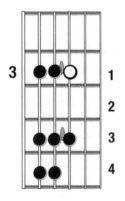

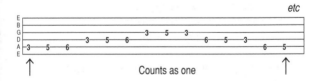

Counts as one

What You Do

Sing the missing note! This is the C minor scale with one of its notes whited out on the fretboard diagram. First, play the scale and listen to the note in question. The next time you play through it, miss out the note on the fretboard and try to sing the correct pitch in its place.

Points To Watch

The missing note in this minor scale is the seventh – one of the more important members of the unit, because it is often included in minor chords (ie C min7). Take a while to familiarise yourself fully with its sound before trying to build up any speed in the workout.

How It Benefits You

Chord tones have special significance in any scale because they become focal points for the ear during solos – they are, literally, safe notes to play – so becoming accustomed to how the minor seventh sounds will bode well for your musical future!

Standard	Number Of Repeats In Two Minutes
Beginner	4–9
Intermediate	10–30
Advanced	31–55

WORKOUT 21

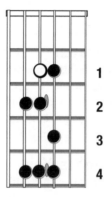

1
2
3
4

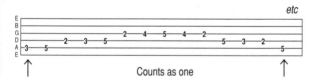

etc

Counts as one

What You Do

Sing the missing note! This is the C major scale with one of its notes whited out on the fretboard diagram. First, play the scale and listen to the notes in question. The next time you play through it, miss out the note on the fretboard and try to sing the correct pitch in its place.

Points To Watch

The note that's gone AWOL is the third – one of the strongest scale and chord tones in the whole music business. Playing the scale itself will present only very minor problems, as the fingering is dead straightforward, so this will leave you absolutely free to concentrate on the job in hand.

How It Benefits You

As I said, the third is very important in music, so it's vital that you're aware not only of its presence on the fretboard but of its aural positioning amongst the other scale tones, too.

Standard	Number Of Repeats In Two Minutes
Beginner	4–8
Intermediate	9–26
Advanced	27–45

WORKOUT 22

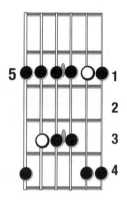

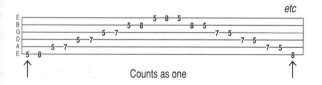

Counts as one

What You Do

Sing the missing notes! This is the A minor pentatonic scale with two of its notes whited out on the diagram. First, play the scale and listen to the notes in question. The next time you play it, miss out the notes on the fretboard and try to sing the correct pitches in their place.

Points To Watch

The note that's taken a leave of absence here is the fifth (one per octave), one of the principal chord tones in music and, therefore, of great musical importance. It might be helpful to play the missing notes over a few times to familiarise yourself with its sound before trying to wrap the scale around it in this workout.

How It Benefits You

The root, third and fifth notes of any scale are of great musical significance as they not only form the tonic chord of that scale but are also the centres of gravity around which a great deal of improvisation is based. Trust me.

Standard	Number Of Repeats In Two Minutes
Beginner	2–6
Intermediate	7–25
Advanced	26–50

WORKOUT 23

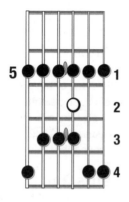

etc

Counts as one

What You Do

A variation on the sing-the-missing-note theme. The scale is shown in full with the whited-out note added. The idea is to play through the scale and try to sing the note that connects the two on the G string. Play the white note first to prepare your ear and then just go for it!

Points To Watch

The note that's grafted onto the A *minor* pentatonic is the *major* third. In blues-based music, the exact musical 'gender' of this oft-used scale is a little confused, in that it's neither truly major nor minor. Using this workout, your ear will be exposed to the effect of both major and minor thirds within the context of the scale.

How It Benefits You

The musical implications here are really quite significant, although the theoretical explanation (an attempted summary of which is shown above) might still elude you. Stick with it, though – it's doing you good.

Standard	Number Of Repeats In Two Minutes
Beginner	2–6
Intermediate	7–25
Advanced	26–50

WORKOUT 24

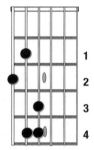

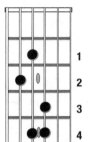

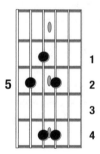

Counts as one

What You Do

Play three arpeggios: G maj7, C maj7 and D7. There's one position change and some fairly straight fingering.

Points To Watch

The only technical obstacle here is the position change and the fact that the third arpeggio has a slightly different fingering to the other two. You may find that your third finger wants to join in the fun on the third because it's been called upon previously. Try to deny it its fun and let finger 2 take the strain.

How It Benefits You

This is a very common chord arrangement played in arpeggio form. Getting to know its inner voicing is great for the ear and bound to benefit you in the future.

Standard	Number Of Repeats In Two Minutes
Beginner	4–8
Intermediate	9–30
Advanced	31–55

WORKOUT 25

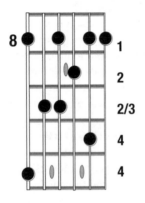

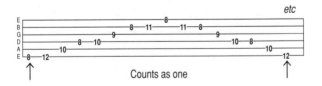

Counts as one

What You Do

A two-octave C7 arpeggio with no position changes. Note how this exercise resembles the C7 barre chord. Here, we're tying together visual and aural reference points.

Points To Watch

There's a stretch for the left hand fourth finger to begin with, which could pose a technical challenge. I've offered an optional fingering for the notes on the fifth and fourth strings; the exercise is possible using finger 3 for both notes at the tenth fret. However, if your hand is out of position because of stretching to reach for the second note on the bass E with finger 4, it might be faster to use finger 2 for the note at the tenth fret on the fifth string instead. Try both and see which feels right for you.

How It Benefits You

This is one of the more common chords literally broken down to its component parts so that the ear has the best possible chance of absorbing everything that's going on.

Standard	Number Of Repeats In Two Minutes
Beginner	4–8
Intermediate	9–26
Advanced	27–50

WORKOUT 26

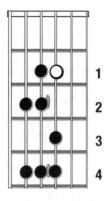

Counts as one

What You So

Sing the missing note! This is the C major scale with one of its notes whited out on the fretboard diagram. First, play the scale and listen to the note in question. The next time you play through it, miss out the note on the fretboard and try to sing the correct pitch in its place.

Points To Watch

It's the sixth note of the scale that's gone missing here. It's reasonably difficult to pitch, not being one of the more common chord tones, but the sixth is an important interval in music and a lot of different styles have employed its charms somewhere along the way. There are no technical difficulties here; just concentrate on pitching that sixth!

How It Benefits You

Becoming familiar with the positions of all scale tones is one of the fundamental ear-training skills to master, especially with the major scale.

Standard	Number Of Repeats In Two Minutes
Beginner	4–9
Intermediate	10–28
Advanced	29–60

WORKOUT 27

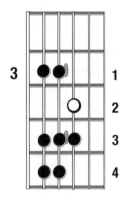

What You Do

This is the harmonic minor scale with one of its notes whited out. Play through the complete scale a couple of times to familiarise yourself with the slightly unusual flavour of the missing note, then play the scale again with the note missing and try to hum or sing it instead.

Points To Watch

Although less common than the natural minor (the one in use in a lot of rock and pop music), the harmonic minor still crops quite often, right across the style spectrum. The missing note is the seventh, a note responsible for giving the scale it's 'Eastern' sound. It's a hard one to pitch accurately, but spend the next two minutes trying.

How It Benefits You

Sampling some of the vast array of alternative tonalities in music is what ear training is really all about. The way in which this particular note integrates with the harmonic minor is the key to this particular scale's identity.

Standard	Number Of Repeats In Two Minutes
Beginner	4–9
Intermediate	10–28
Advanced	29–55

WORKOUT 28

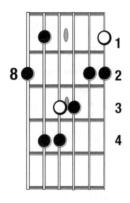

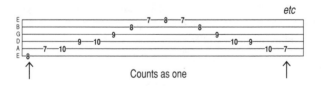

Counts as one

What You Do

Here's a major-seventh arpeggio over two octaves in a single position with two notes whited out. Play the complete arpeggio to begin with, then play it again, missing out the white notes and singing them instead.

Points To Watch

Someone once told me that the major seventh – the missing note here – is one of the most difficult intervals for a singer to pitch accurately. Luckily, we're not here because of our singing abilities, but you still might have difficulty filling in the blanks. Watch the fingering – a little orienteering is probably called for before you start building speed. Keep an eye on what the right hand gets up to, as well!

How It Benefits You

This is another very common chord form, with its innards on display to give your ear a chance to hear what's going on.

Standard	Number Of Repeats In Two Minutes
Beginner	4–8
Intermediate	9–25
Advanced	26–55

WORKOUT 29

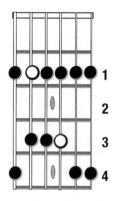

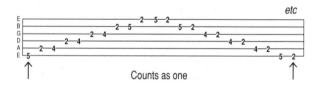

Counts as one

What You Do

Sing the missing notes! This is the A major pentatonic scale with two of its notes whited out. Play the scale and listen to the notes in question, then play it again, miss out the notes and try to sing them instead.

Points To Watch

You're vocalising the second, and the scale that's wrapped around it should be a familiar one, as both major and minor scales share the same shapes. So there should be only a minimal amount of technical difficulty involved in overcoming this workout, leaving you free to focus on how the second sounds.

How It Benefits You

Notes within a scale have a sort of hierarchy that comes into force during improvisation. Chord tones are of the most importance, with scale tones rattling along behind. Becoming familiar with some of these lesser scale members is still vital information for the ear.

Standard	Number Of Repeats In Two Minutes
Beginner	2–6
Intermediate	7–25
Advanced	26–40

WORKOUT 30

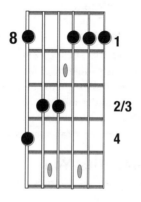

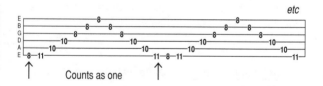

etc

Counts as one

What You Do

Play this C minor arpeggio over two octaves, in a single position.

Points To Watch

The fingering for the notes on the fifth and fourth strings needs careful attention. I would advise you to begin this scale using fingers 1, 4, 2, 3 and so on. This will produce more fluency than trying to play two successive notes with the same finger. Other than that, notice how similar this arpeggio is to a C minor barre chord. It's a very important visual reference that will hopefully become an aural reference point, too!

How It Benefits You

The benefits of hearing chords played one note at a time (which is essentially what an arpeggio is) are manifold and your ear will thank you for it in the long run!

Standard	Number Of Repeats In Two Minutes
Beginner	6–12
Intermediate	13–30
Advanced	31–60

WORKOUT 31

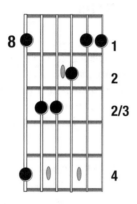

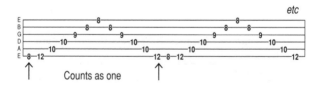

etc

Counts as one

What You Do

Here's a C major arpeggio at the eighth fret, spanning two octaves, with no position changes – just that initial big stretch on the bass string followed by an alternate-fingering strategy on the fifth and fourth strings.

Points To Watch

It may be difficult to stretch your fourth finger far enough without moving your hand, but this will interrupt the flow of the exercise, so persevere. After stretching the fourth finger to play the note at fret 12, your hand should already be extended to accommodate fingering the note at the tenth fret on the fifth string with finger 2. If you aim to do this on the return journey, too, your hand will find that sixth-string stretch that much easier.

How It Benefits You

Every style of music is drenched with mainly major harmony, so an aural snapshot of the harmonic mechanism at work is priceless for the ear.

Standard	Number Of Repeats In Two Minutes
Beginner	4–10
Intermediate	11–40
Advanced	41–66

WORKOUT 32

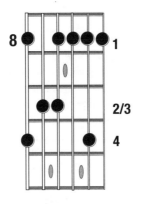

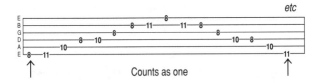

Counts as one

What You Do

Here's a C minor-seventh arpeggio that looks uncannily like a scale – two octaves, no position changes, but a slightly unorthodox fingering for string 5.

Points To Watch

See how much this arpeggio looks like a minor pentatonic scale? Now you can see why that scale fits so readily over minor-sounding chords! I'd advise you to play the fifth string with finger 2, as this should keep things flowing more than trying to play both of the notes at the tenth fret, fifth and fourth strings, with finger 3. Otherwise, there are no technical traps. Just keep an eye on the right hand and make sure your picking is alternate.

How It Benefits You

There should be a fair amount of subliminal information being fed to the head here. The way in which the minor-seventh arpeggio contains nearly all of the notes from the minor pentatonic is no coincidence, after all!

Standard	Number Of Repeats In Two Minutes
Beginner	4–8
Intermediate	9–30
Advanced	31–60

WORKOUT 33

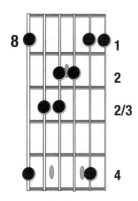

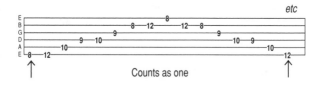

Counts as one

What You Do

Here's a C major arpeggio over two octaves with a couple of nasty stretches for poor old finger 4!

Points To Watch

The left-hand fingering may cause some concern here. The exercise starts off with quite a wide stretch for the fourth finger, and you should play the note at the tenth fret on the fifth string with the second finger. This should aid the overall flow of the arpeggio, as you'll find finger 2 hanging around here, in any case, due to the fourth-finger stretch. There's another perilous-looking reach for finger 4 on the second string, too. Once again, try not to let the hand wander out of position, as this can slow things down.

How It Benefits You

The major seventh is an important chord and used quite frequently in all types of music. Feeding its signature sound directly into your ear will do you a lot of good.

Standard	Number Of Repeats In Two Minutes
Beginner	4–8
Intermediate	9–25
Advanced	26–55

WORKOUT 34

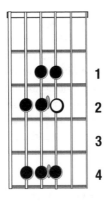

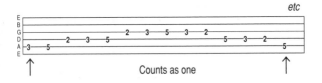

Counts as one

What You Do

Sing the missing note! This is the C dominant-seventh scale with one of its notes whited out on the fretboard diagram. First, play the scale and listen to the note in question. The next time you play through it, miss out the note on the fretboard and try to sing the correct pitch in its place.

Points To Watch

This is fairly easy, technically speaking. The missing note is the dominant seventh itself – the note that gives this scale its basic flavour. It's also an important chord tone and therefore a good one to try to pitch. The third finger can take a quick rest during this workout.

How It Benefits You

Dominant-seventh scales turn up in blues- and jazz-related music all the time, so the dominant seventh is a really important note to commit to memory.

Standard	Number Of Repeats In Two Minutes
Beginner	4–8
Intermediate	9–30
Advanced	31–65

WORKOUT 35

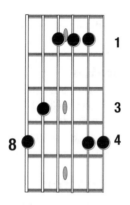

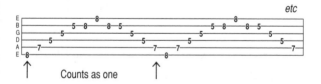

Counts as one

What You Do

Here's an alternative shape for a C major arpeggio. It looks familiar because of its close resemblance to a chord of G.

Points To Watch

This is, in fact, one of the barre shapes available for C major at the fifth fret, but it's rarely played because it's awkward to finger, although it makes a good arpeggio study, all the same. Finger 1 can remain in position as you play all the notes on the D, G and B strings. In fact, if you can leave it there longer, do so, because it will help speed things up no end. Watch your picking, too; don't get fooled into thinking you're strumming a chord. You're not, so alternate picking is still the house rule.

How It Benefits You

Hearing chords broken down to individual notes will do your ear an awful lot of good. Try humming along so that this vital information becomes really embedded.

Standard	Number Of Repeats In Two Minutes
Beginner	5–10
Intermediate	11–40
Advanced	41–70

WORKOUT 36

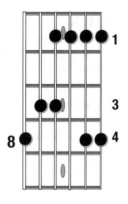

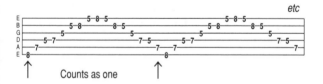

etc

Counts as one

What You Do

Play this C major-sixth arpeggio, which is an almost Identikit fit for a common scale shape.

Points To Watch

If you're thinking that this arpeggio looks remarkably like a C major pentatonic scale, then reward yourself heartily, because you're dead right! Try to lay the first-finger barre for as long as possible in both directions (ie going up and coming down the arpeggio), as this will help you speed things up significantly. Apart from that, there are no real technical problems here at all.

How It Benefits You

This exercise really helps to underline the similarity between a chord shape (in the form of an arpeggio) and a scale shape. This all gets stored in your memory banks and will pop up when you least expect it one day when you're called on to play a solo.

Standard	Number Of Repeats In Two Minutes
Beginner	4–8
Intermediate	9–30
Advanced	31–55

WORKOUT 37

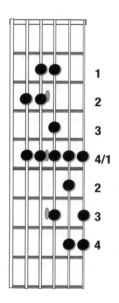

Counts as one

What You Do

Here's a C major scale spanning two octaves and two positions, with a few fingering issues along the way.

Points To Watch

For this workout, you need to be familiar with the left-hand fingering before you can expect any degree of fluency while playing it. The exact point to change is on the third string, after having played the note at the fourth fret with your third finger. Play the note at the fifth fret with your first finger and the rest of the exercise will be in reach. Reverse everything on the way down and things should flow smoothly. Watch the right hand and make sure it's doing its alternate picking correctly – mistakes take ages to put right if not caught in the early stages.

How It Benefits You

Any way the major scale is presented on the fretboard is worth mastering. This exercise represents an important set of aural landmarks for your developing sense of music.

Standard	Number Of Repeats In Two Minutes
Beginner	1–4
Intermediate	5–20
Advanced	21–34

WORKOUT 38

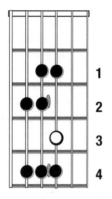

1

2

3

4

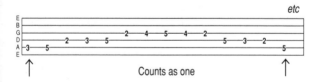

etc

Counts as one

What You Do

Sing the missing note! This is the C major scale with one of its notes whited out. Play the scale and listen, then play again and sing the missing note, as before.

Points To Watch

There are a lot of very similar exercises in this section, so my guess is that you've encountered the sing-the-missing-note game a few times before. The rules don't change, but the notes and their context within the scale certainly do! In this instance, the note that's been whited out is the major seventh, an important scale tone and quite often a chord tone, too. Here, all four fingers are called into play – at least, until you start missing out finger 3 and humming the pitch instead.

How It Benefits You

Pounding the information contained in the major scale into the ear is incredibly valuable. Finding the missing note with your voice helps immeasurably, too.

Standard	Number Of Repeats In Two Minutes
Beginner	4–9
Intermediate	10–40
Advanced	41–65

WORKOUT 39

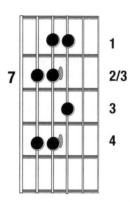

Counts as one

What You Do

Here's an E major scale at the seventh fret with a repetitive, alternating pedal (a continual pitch against which a melody line is played, remember?) in the bass.

Points To Watch

Although this is a major-scale shape you might have encountered before, playing it through in this fashion might present you with a few unexpected technical hitches. It's a good thing to anchor your second finger on the seventh fret, fifth string, and play around it. This means that the seventh fret, fourth string, has to be played by the third finger, and this might feel wrong at first, but you'll soon get used to it. In the field, you have to make changes to your fingering patterns all the time.

How It Benefits You

The major scale is presented here in yet another way, with the major seventh first instead of the octave – another chance for the brain to re-evaluate its scale-tone data bank!

Standard	Number Of Repeats In Two Minutes
Beginner	5–10
Intermediate	11–45
Advanced	46–70

WORKOUT 40

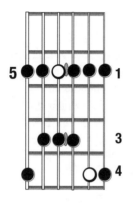

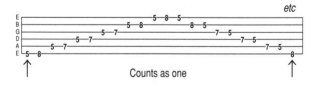

Counts as one

What You Do

Sing the missing notes! This is the A minor pentatonic scale with two of its notes whited out. Play and then sing the missing notes in the scale as before.

Points To Watch

In this variation on our sing-the-missing-note game, it's the minor scale's flat seventh that's been whited out. This is, without doubt, one of the grittiest notes in the scale and it's therefore very good to focus the ear on it. Nothing too technically demanding here. Let the second finger put its feet up for the duration. After Chapter 2, it probably needs the rest!

How It Benefits You

This is a very common scale in all blues-related music (and that's just about everything modern) laid bare, leaving the ear having to fill in a couple of vital blanks. Nothing could be better training for your aural skills.

Standard	Number Of Repeats In Two Minutes
Beginner	2–6
Intermediate	7–24
Advanced	25–40

APPENDIX
Expert Insight

This section contains quotes from interviews I conducted during my tenure as a guitar-magazine editor. They are all meant to inspire, amuse, surprise, gently cajole or just generally refresh you after your time in the guitar gym!

'The guitar is so difficult to get your own sound on and, if I've come up with my own sound, I think it's been by luck. It's just sort of been shaped over a long period of time' *John Scofield*

'When we first started recording, there were no effects available; you just plugged in. I think I did the first couple of albums on an old Fender Tweed concert amp and you plugged the Gibson SG or Flying-V into that, turned it up to three-quarters volume and there was your distortion.' *Andy Powell, from Wishbone Ash*

'The bottleneck I carry with me is the one I made in 1967. I use the neck from a Mateus Rosé wine bottle, but unfortunately they changed the bottle in 1973 and so they're not as good any more. Every once in a while, you'll go into something of a hippie environment and see one being used as a candleholder. Hold it up to the light and if there's a bluish cast to it, it's pre-1973.' *Bob Brozman*

'You never can learn enough with any instrument. I don't practise as much as I used to, but when I was really into my late teens and early 20s I kept a guitar by the bed with the radio turned down real low. Nobody would hear it except me, and every time a guitar would come on and you'd hear something, you'd grab the damned guitar right then and get as near to what you heard as you could. If you could sleep with that guitar in your hand, it wouldn't be too much guitar.' *Buddy Guy*

'Until we can ask our bodies to do nothing for a short time, we can't really ask our bodies to do something quite specific for a short time.' *Robert Fripp*

'If we can say we've got two or three million fans in England, that means there are 57 million people who don't give a shit!' *Francis Rossi*

'A guitar is so temperamental, anything you change on it will change the sound. You change the pick guard and it makes a difference.' *Steve Vai*

'Back when people wanted to put me on the cover for being a technical guitar hero, I would say, "Please, that's not what I do. I write songs, I believe in beautiful instrumental music and that's my focus. If you want to ask me what sort of string I use or how many hours I practise, I'll go through it, but that's not really what I do."' *Joe Satriani*

'When it comes to teaching, I'm all in favour of understanding and learning certain factual things to do with style, but I think, beyond that, you'd be better off to take as a model either jazz or folk music and try to play with the idiom or style but let the interpretation be totally personal.' *Classical guitar maestro John Williams*

'I would sooner use the time I have practising something I'm going to use rather than doing gymnastics or exercises, so now I never play scales or anything like that.' *Martin Taylor*

'I listen to my favourite records that I used to look to when I first got excited about it all now and again. The hardest thing to get out of those records is why they play the way they do – the emotion behind it, the passion and so on. I think you have to listen to a record and grab hold of that spirit and then it takes you to how, why and what made them play the notes that they do, whether it's a flurry or whether it's one pretty singing note just to put a dab of colour on a piece of paper. If you listen to a song that way and try to play it that way, it's magical. That's where you get that spirit from.'
Robert Cray

'I was around 15 when I first heard bottleneck slide on record, which totally amazed me, and I fell in love with the sound. Once I heard Robert Johnson, that inspired me to combine his style with Chet Atkins' fingerstyle. I put the two together and that was a big step for me.' Sonny Landreth

'A lot of the single lines that I put in between the phrases are very much my way of improvising. I had done so much work in D during the psychedelic era that when I came to improvise in D I had a huge array of things I could do. I'd spent so long droning away in Indian improvisation!' *Steve Howe*

'I started out just being the guitarist in a band. I was never the centre figure – that came later – and I always enjoyed that spot, being just the guitarist. I wanted to be the Hank Marvin of my time.' *Peter Frampton*

'He plays the perfect note over the weirdest chord, y'know?' *Steve Lukather on Larry Carlton*

'I think it takes patience, big ears and a lack of ego.' *Larry Carlton on playing with other musicians*

'You just do the next thing. The terms "bigger" or "better" don't really mean anything. You just do the best you can at any given moment.' *Pink Floyd's David Gilmour*

'The good thing about being well prepared is that you might get a night where you're uninspired or not feeling up to it and you can just engage autopilot. Then you just go to what you've rehearsed and that's going be good enough.' *Dominic Miller, from Sting's band*

'Life is a blur once rehearsals start. I remember the first tour was a solid month of the band in one room, the singers in another and the dancers in another... The second month was full production with pyro and Michael and everything together on a huge soundstage.' *Jennifer Batten remembering touring in Michael Jackson's band*

'The trick is to be as consistent as possible all the time. It's the complete antithesis of a club gig, where the excitement of the moment is shared by people close to you. A big show is a big machine and you're a very small element.' *David Rhodes, from Peter Gabriel's band*

'I use a thumb pick, a finger pick and my third finger as well. I used to use two fingerpicks, but I would always lose the third one in the soundhole and the guitar ended up becoming a giant maraca.' *John Hammond*

'When I was 14 or 15, I left home. I just took off, you know? I didn't want to stay in the South and work on the farm. I figured there had to be a better way in the world and I headed north. Then, when I recorded "Boogie Chillun'", I got a hit on it.' *John Lee Hooker*

basic Guitar Workout

'I use an 11–52 string gauge... I can bend the 12 up a minor third pretty easily. I don't have any problem, as I've pretty strong fingers.' *Robbie McIntosh, from Paul McCartney's band*

'I used to borrow acoustic guitars and ended up learning fingerstyle.' *Mark Knopfler*

'I gave up ruining records trying to work out every note Robert Johnson played, but during the years all of this listening has really started to come back into the writing. I think basically that that's the way to go.' *Eric Bibb*

'As a teenager, all I wanted to do was play jazz.' *Andy Summers, from The Police*

'There's not much for me to do up front. Even then it's like crossing the M40, what with Brian and Angus out there.' *Onstage with AC/DC's Malcolm Young*

'It's not about technique. It's not about what kind of instrument you play or how many strings it's got or how fast you can play or how loud it is or how quiet it is. It's about how it feels and how it makes you feel when you play.' *Eric Clapton*

'You don't have to be black and broke to have the blues... You can be Jewish and have nice cars.' *Leslie West*

'I think the general thing is to practise as much as you can, play with other musicians as much as you can – especially drummers, because it helps your timing – and use your ears. If something sounds bad, try and figure out what it is.' *Paul Gilbert*

'Listen to the past. I've run into a lot of players in the last 10 or 15 years who don't really know where it was coming from – they thought it came from Jimmy Page or they thought it came from Jeff Beck or they thought it came from Buddy Guy or that it came from BB King. Well, it comes from further back, and if you go back and listen to Robert Johnson and Blind Blake and Blind Boy Fuller and Blind Willie Johnson and Blind Willie McTell, there's thousands of them that all have something which led to where it is now. The beauty of it is that you can take one of those things and make it yours. But by learning too much from the later players, you don't have that much opportunity to make something original. I listened to King Oliver and I listened to Louis Armstrong and I listened to Thelonious Monk and I listened to Charles Mingus and I listened to John Coltrane and I listened to Archie Shepp. I listened to everything I could that came from that place that they call the blues but in formality isn't necessarily the blues.' *Eric Clapton*

'Pieces of music have harmony, melody and rhythm and some sort of idea that makes them go. The rest is just a matter of orchestration.' *Frank Zappa*

'If I can think of a guitar part but I can't actually do it as well as I'd like to hear it done, then I'll get someone else who can.' *David Gilmour*

8/09(170487)